15892.
23/4/65

e o

3 C

2   11 5·65

16/—

5 AUG

21 AU

17 SEP

15 OC   3

Cities of the World:

CAIRO

Cities of the World:

CAIRO

DESMOND STEWART

with 24 photographs and 2 maps

PHOENIX HOUSE
London

By the same author
Fiction

LEOPARD IN THE GRASS

THE UNSUITABLE ENGLISHMAN

A WOMAN BESIEGED

Non-Fiction

NEW BABYLON, A PORTRAIT OF IRAQ
(with John Haylock)

YOUNG EGYPT

TURMOIL IN BEIRUT

THE ARAB WORLD
(Life World Library)

Cover illustration: *The great early medieval
walls of Fatimid Cairo*

Contents

List of Illustrations
and Maps

(Except where otherwise stated, photographs are by Mr Sayid Hassan.)

vii

Note

THE transliteration of Arabic—the writing of Arabic words in Latin letters—has always been a problem to European writers. Arabic has a number of consonants for which English has no equivalent. An important example is the *'Ain*, the throat-gulp which precedes 'Ali or 'Iraq. This letter is usually written as a rough breathing, or omitted altogether. In addition to *kaf*, a letter corresponding to the English 'k', Arabic has another, harder form of the same sound, *qaf*, farther back in the throat. To find exact equivalents for these consonants has always been a problem when transliterating the classical language. I will cite only one example: the Fatimid Caliph who founded the third Muslim city on the site of Cairo is described in *The Shorter Encyclopaedia of Islam* as *Ma'add*, while writers such as Stanley Lane Poole who follow Egyptian pronunciation call him Mo'izz. The problem is yet severer in writing about modern Cairo, a bustling quotidian city where people no more talk in classical Arabic than Londoners talk in Miltonian English. Cairenes drop the *qaf* much as Cockneys drop the aitch. Thus, *qahwah*, coffee, is pronounced as *ahwah*; the word for citadel, *qal'ah*, is pronounced *al'ah*; in both cases, it should be added, the final 'h' is silent and is often omitted, as I have done in this book. To compound the difficulty, when Cairo's streets were labelled with signs in Arabic and Latin letters, the dominant cultural influence was French. Thus, the definite article ﻝ was generally transliterated as *el*, while in those parts of the Arab world where English influence was dominant the transliteration was *al*. Egyptian journals printed in English frequently transliterate the same name in several different ways

within one article. If in this book I have been similarly haphazard
I can plead that, where there is no undisputed orthography,
mistakes are venial. In every case I have tried to write Arabic
names with the minimum of fuss, so that those who visit Cairo
will produce on foreign lips an approximation to the word
required.

Chapter 1

Desert

CAIRO, the largest of desert cities,[1] has a desert colour. It was formed by a desert faith. The best approach is from the desert: a motor road from the Mediterranean runs for 130 miles through undulant beige wilderness till it swoops up behind the Pyramids and descends into a valley oasis, its course shimmered over by a metropolis of grey and brown. Even aeroplanes do not avoid this clash of life with death. They approach their runway over dunes of sand.

Cairo is built out of the desert to which it clings. The wondrous triangles erected by Cheops and his heirs were composed from millions of blocks of sandstone first quarried from the Mokattam hills and then floated west across the valley, over the site of the present city, when the river was in flood. Later these convenient blocks of congealed desert were used for the mosques and palaces of Muslim rulers.

Much of the city has returned to the desert of the past. The Golden Hall where the Caliph Al-Moʻizz surveyed court festivals from behind a screen of golden filigree has vanished with the four thousand rooms of the palace, with the bones of the Greek and Sudanese slaves who did his bidding. Nothing remains of the Emerald Hall or the Great Divan. Clinging to the hills from which the Pyramids came and from which at dawn the sun greets the western Sphinx stand ruined mosques like the unfinished reveries in some Gothic tale.

The desert invades the city, whether the boulevards of the new

[1] 414 sq. kms.; population, 1964, estimated 3,348,000.

quarters or the twisting alleys of the old. In May the *khamsin*, blowing from Libya, carries a fine dust that seeps through the tightest windows, that leaves vegetation and architecture greyly powdered. The long Egyptian eyelashes are weapons against this dust, not ornaments.

The delights of Cairo, like those of the desert, are the sharper for their dusty background. Stalls sell mango juice or the sap of sugarcane to cool violent thirsts. Flowers make vivid colour points in drab corners. When on a hot day the sun at last sinks behind the Hilton, a unique perfume, in part of lilies, in part of leopards, pervades the pavements.

Deserts, like seas, are more than vacuums. They are forces that join. Just as seas linked the Greek cities of the ancient Mediterranean, so deserts joined the distant regions of the Middle East. Travellers and tourists have come to the site of Cairo from the start of history. For though Cairo takes its name from Arabic, its site was important long before the Arabs left Arabia. Here where the Nile broadens into the fan-shaped Delta, the Pharaohs built their capital of Memphis. (The stepped Pyramid of Sakkara, the world's oldest stone-built edifice, still dominates the Memphis cemeteries. It is visible from Cairo's higher buildings.) The Pharaohs' chief necropolis was on the plateau of Giza, now reached in forty minutes by a No. 8 bus from Liberation Square (Midan al-Tahrir). At the 'Source of the Sun' (in Arabic *Ain Shems*), the modern Heliopolis, was an ancient place of learning where Herodotus and Plato were instructed by Egyptian priests. Now linked by Metro, Ain Shems gives its name to one of Cairo's four universities.

The most influential travellers brought, not merchandise, but religious ideas. Cairo—like many cities it is only the most recent in a sequence of human habitations—is littered with the physical evidence of religious faiths.

Although the Hebrews (the *Beni Isra'il* of the Koran) did their brick-making in the eastern Delta, the centuries preceding the

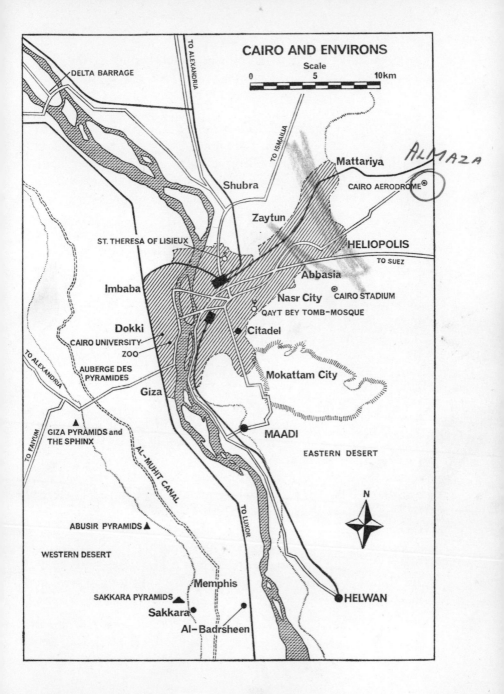

CAIRO AND ENVIRONS

Scale

0   5   10km

ALMAZA

DELTA BARRAGE

TO ALEXANDRIA

TO ISMAILIA

Mattariya

CAIRO AERODROME ⊚

Shubra

Zaytun

HELIOPOLIS

ST. THERESA OF LISIEUX

TO SUEZ

Imbaba

Abbasia

Nasr City

CAIRO STADIUM ⊚

QAYT BEY TOMB-MOSQUE

Dokki

Citadel

CAIRO UNIVERSITY

ZOO

AUBERGE DES
PYRAMIDES

Mokattam City

Giza

TO ALEXANDRIA

GIZA PYRAMIDS and
THE SPHINX

MAADI

EASTERN DESERT

AL-MUHIT CANAL

TO FAIYUM

TO LUXOR

N

ABUSIR PYRAMIDS ▲

WESTERN DESERT

Memphis

SAKKARA PYRAMIDS ▲

Sakkara

HELWAN

Al-Badrsheen

birth of Christ saw Jewish colonies established along the Nile. The largest was near the river's western mouth, at Alexandria. There Philo expounded his monotheism in the terms of Hellenic philosophy. His theory of the *Logos*, or 'Word', was adopted by the Church to explain the Incarnation. Yet it was to the Roman city on the site of Cairo, 'Babylon in Egypt', that the Holy Family, fearing the wrath of Herod, came from Palestine. Coptic monks still show the visitor to their Abu Sarga church, a dank crypt in which the *Logos* and His guardians slept. Nearby is a synagogue with a precious *torah*.

But neither churches nor synagogues rule Cairo's skyline. For this is neither a Jewish nor a Christian city. It is a Muslim *medina*, formed by the faith of Muhammad the Arab, cherished by Muslims as a city hardly less sacred than Mecca, to which the Cairo mosques are oriented, or Medina, the city where Muhammad is buried. And although since 1952 the horizon has been increasingly punctuated by skyscrapers and other angular adornments, the distinctive features of the dun roofscape remain the minarets, symbols of the faith proclaimed five times a day from platforms near their tops.

Cairo, as a desert city in Africa, has distinctive vegetation: flowers that in the north need hothouses, trees that bring flamboyance to arid backgrounds, scaly eucalyptuses with their rustling tinny leaves, acacias that rejoice in drought, the Egyptian sycamore, palms under which the Koran set the Nativity, and the great Bengal figs, or *banians*, whose gloomy branches trail suckers that turn into new dark trees. Since it rains only a few months each year, Cairo green is always overlaid with beige.

Yet, more than its buildings and its vegetation, what makes this desert city unique is the river that gives it life. Other oasis cities are limited by thirst. Cairo's desert is split by the longest river in the Old World, that brings with it donations from the Atlantic via the jungles and mountains of central Africa.

Chapter 2

Nilotic

EVER since Vichy water ceased being imported, every Cairene—
and every visitor—must drink the Nile, river of clichés. 'Who
drinks it once will drink it again.' Yet truer, 'Who drinks it often
can hardly bear to leave it.' To the Egyptian *fellahin*, its water,
however muddy, has a saving blessedness. People cling to this
river. To leave it is agony.

This last sentence is not rhetoric. If you wandered ten miles
east or west of the ribbon of water, you would die of thirst—
unless rescued by Bedouin or a team prospecting for petrol.
Rainfall is minimal; without the Nile Cairo would be one more
anonymous stretch in a desert that sweeps uninterrupted from the
Red Sea mountains through the Sahara to the Atlantic.

The truest cliché of the Nile is the one embodied in its colour.
It shimmers greeny brown like a dowager's silk ball-dress: *eau de
nil*—except when early sun makes it a skein of peacock, or at midnight when there's a glint of metal.

One thing it is not is changeless. Like everything else, its course
has been touched by time. The touch in its case has been disci-
plinary, overruling the dramatic fluctuations of the past. For the
flow of the Nile is the aorta of Egypt. One of the first things built
by the Arabs when they Islamized Egypt was the Nilometer on
the southern tip of Roda island, still visible under a modern
canopy. (The Pharaohs had had their own Nilometers, in Luxor
and elsewhere.) The Nilometer is a deep stone-lined well with a
carved central column crowned with a Corinthian capital and
marked out in cubits. Watching the Nilometer was more urgent

than the Western weather-guessing before bank holidays. On the amount of water in the shaft depended dearth or plenty.

Late August is the time when the flood is expected from inner Africa. The whole city would go out to greet the waters in a ceremony called in Arabic *wafaa al-Nil*, 'the faithfulness of the Nile'. In seasons when the Nile seemed faithless, long praying processions left the streets of east-bank Cairo, headed by the Sultan. He would be followed by the chief dignitaries of Islam, the Coptic priests and the Jewish rabbis, all united in invoking their separate holy books that the Nile be plenteous. Even earlier, the Pharaohs had surmised that the flood waters were the tears of Isis mourning for Osiris. A savage rite of ancient times survived transmogrified: that of casting *arousat al-Nil*, 'the bride of the Nile', to her riverine lover—originally a living maiden, like one of the Athenian girls sent to the horns of the Minotaur; later a life-sized doll.

Now that dams control the Nile, there is no longer the July wasting followed by the dramatic revivification of rat-ruled mud-banks. There are no more aquatic processions to greet the floods. Now the river swells a little in late summer; the Cairenes complain of humidity added to heat; the rich ones escape to Alexandria—also humid, but more breezy. The mosquitoes multiply.

The Nile's course has altered with time. With it its facilities have altered too.

The earliest port for the east-bank city (Memphis lay on the west bank) was near the Roman Babylon, to the south of the modern city. In the early Middle Ages the port was Maks, near the Continental Hotel and Azbakiya Gardens of today. The business and entertainment section, the *art nouveau* streets west of the line from the station at Bab al-Hadid through Azbakiya to Bab al-Louk was an area of orchards and gardens in the early nineteenth century, flooded each summer. The Azbakiya Gardens (now diminished by town planning) were in the eighteenth century a lake; by Napoleon's time they were sufficiently dry for him to review his troops there. Bab al-Louk, with market and suburban station, in the Middle Ages was a river-gate. As the Nile bed shifted, Maks yielded to Bulak, emerging with its island, the Gezira, from the river. Bulak is now as blurred in the fabric of Cairo as Chelsea is in London's. Yet in the time of Napoleon it was still the port of Cairo. To those disembarking the capital was invisible from Bulak on account of the mountain-like rubbish dumps between the city walls and the river.

Water has not merely changed its course; it has been overlaid by concrete, just as the rubbish dumps have been overclimbed by houses, or in some cases, planted with trees.

Until the turn of the present century a canal flowed through the heart of Cairo. This canal, or *khalig*, was the first beneficiary of the annual flood. Water rushed into it from the Nile, near the ruined aqueduct and up through the Mousky, lending the overhanging houses the aroma, in every sense, of an oriental Venice. This canal was the survivor of the *amnis* of the Roman emperor Trajan. It linked the Nile valley with the gulf of Suez through the eastern Delta. Fallen into disuse, it was restored by Amr (first Muslim ruler of Egypt) so that he could export the wheat of the Nile valley to Arabia. It is now, after the riverside *corniche*, the longest thoroughfare in Cairo. A broad, rather ugly road with tall aluminium lamp-posts, its name has been changed from Shari Khalig al-Masri, or 'street of the Egyptian canal', to Shari Port-Said. Street names change more quickly than any river.

In the early nineteenth century the Nile, like the Bosphorus, was a sinister oubliette into which rebellious subjects might be thrown, trussed bridegrooms of a sexually ambiguous river. The Nile has lost this sinister association. Now it is a gentle motif in a city which is otherwise harsh.

Outside the Semiramis dark boatmen await the invitation of those, Egyptian or foreign, who want a *felucca*. The boatmen often come from Aswan, far to the south. They charge about five shillings for an hour's sail. You walk along a rickety gangplank. Petrol fumes and noise are suddenly remote. The tattered but expertly manipulated sail fills and there is the fast lapping of water as the *felucca*, its shape eternal as the river, skims past the University Hospital (Kasr al-Aini) towards University Bridge (Al-Gamia). On feast days and holidays a concrete fountain, embedded in the river by Krupps, the bridge-builders, spouts a skein of water higher than the hotels.

The Nile is unlike that other great Arab river, whose name in Greek meant 'the Tiger'. Where Iraq's Tigris is a rapacious, violent river, flooding at the wrong time—in spring, when the water is not yet needed—the Nile is the most convenient waterway on earth. It is equally convenient for transport and for irrigation. Its steady northward movement carries boats to the Mediterranean. At the same time its dominant wind from the same northern sea makes the return voyage easy, without tacking. Most important, it floods when its water is needed, as summer drought begins to parch the fields.

This gentle element in their desert city is loved by the people of Cairo. The most desirable apartments are those on the river's banks. The new Shepheard's Hotel, removed from its pyre near Azbakiya, takes its place with the Semiramis and the Hilton, looking west over water. Where the Gezira divides the Nile, the western, narrower branch is lined with houseboats, shabbily romantic. (Cairo has 190 houseboats; their major drawback is their openness to mosquitoes.)

The Nile is finally tamed just north of Cairo, at the Barrage. A lengthy wall holds back water against the four thirsty months. It does so with castellated architecture in the style of the Waverley Novels.

The Barrage symbolizes the historical centrality of Cairo. Its position at the apex of the Delta gives it easy control over Upper and Lower Egypt. Whoever controls water in a desert country controls the country. Cairo owes its importance to standing where the one Nile divides into several, the arteries fanning north to feed the Flemish-fertile acres of the Delta. Cairo is not merely a great city: it is a great capital, unquestioned ruler of a nation, but whose people are varied, polychrome.

Chapter 3

Polychrome

CAIRO has been many-coloured since its foundation. Even in the centuries when the House of Islam was cut off from the House of War (or Christendom), different peoples poured into Egypt, including, in 1163, the Crusaders. The changing city was unchanging in this. The white slaves from the Caucasus (who became, as Mamelukes, the rulers), the black slaves from the Sudan (against whose frequent tumult the timid merchants built their studded doors), traders from Java and China, scholars and holy men from Tunis and Morocco; and, more numerous and persistent than these, the Egyptian peasantry from delta and valley, whose blood already carried the chromosomes of Pharaohs, Libyans, Nubians, Greeks, Ethiopians and Somalis. In the caravanserais and colleges of this city the distinctive Cairo variegation was long established. (We may discount, while noting, the generalization published by the editress of Murray's *1896 Hand Book*: 'The town-bred Cairene is much quicker and more intelligent than his country cousin; and he may generally be distinguished by certain outward signs, such as a peculiar tint of tawny complexion, large mouth, with thick well-formed lips, fat broad nose, enormous legs and a general look of sturdiness.')

When Napoleon opened Egypt to Europe, the city's contrasts became more startling. The modern West was added to the immemorial East . . . though not always the West at its best or most honest. Impelled by poverty in southern Europe, waves of migrants invaded nineteenth-century Egypt. The sub-European communities could be numbered by the hundred thousand. To

them were added a *Völkerwanderung* of Levantines, described by
their Egyptian hosts as *Shami*, from an Arabic name for Damascus
which by extension included Syria and Lebanon. These foreigners
did well in Egypt—except physically. As though Nature punished
them with one hand while rewarding them with the other, their
skins developed a greyish pallor less attractive than the darker
skins of those they lived among. But their bank balances were
healthy.

The colloquial name for Cairo is not *Al-Qahira*, but *Masr*,
which in Arabic also means 'Egypt'. Since the revolution of 1952,
tamsir, or Egyptianization, has been part policy, part accident.
The wave of foreigners has receded, pushed back by legislation,
sequestration, nationalism, a change of political climate. The
migrants have been drawn back, too, by the new prosperity in their
countries of origin. Thus, since the revolution, Cairo is a darker
city. It is also less elegant. In the last years of King Farouk the
masses of Egyptians were sunk in a poverty made the less bearable
for a total lack of hope. The burning of Cairo on 26th January
1952 (a petrol station between Adly Street and Sarwat Street has
replaced the burnt-out Turf Club) was not only a protest against
poverty. It was also a protest against an elegance flagrant in the
midst of poverty. For in those dismal days beautiful princesses
would go shopping in Fuad I Street and Suliman Pasha Street, the
luxurious thoroughfares of central Cairo (now renamed 26th July
Street and Talaat Harb Street, and no longer luxurious). Some
restaurants offered snails and exotic cheeses flown in from Paris.
At the same time many Egyptians fed themselves on twopence
halfpenny a day.

The new Cairo has few peaks of elegance. The intention is to
bulldoze the troughs of despair as well.

Yet despite a government whose aim is a more uniform society,
the people of Cairo remain visibly varied. The city itself, in its
quarters as well as its manners, reflects the various races, colours
and customs that compose its people.

Chapter 4

Baladi

THREE Cairo newspapers—*Al-Ahram*, *Al-Akhbar* and *Al-Gumhouriya* [1]—compete but do not quarrel. Their cartoonists usually depict the basic Cairene as a skinny, sometimes bespectacled, always cynical little man with a flowing robe of striped cotton, leather slippers and on his head an untidy turban or white cotton cap. The red *tarbush*—originally a Turkish innovation from North Africa—has been abolished as a symbol of backwardness (only foreign tourists and Nubian waiters retain it). Later Turkish modes are fortunately not fashionable in Cairo. Atatürk's adoption of the proletarian cloth cap has not been copied. Most Cairenes (and practically all Cairo women) go bareheaded.

The adjective used to describe the basic Cairene of the cartoons, and the back-streets, is '*baladi*', literally 'of the village'. *Baladi* can describe either the traditional way of life or the quarters in which it is lived. To the timid foreigner, Egyptians in *gallabya*, raucous-voiced, excitable, exclamatory, may seem incongruous in a metropolis of increasing modernity, even sinister. To those who take the trouble of meeting them (and in their little shops or cafés they are approachable), the *baladi* Cairenes are the salt of the city: unpretentious, spontaneous, humorous, democratic; the older ones are also courtly. Their basic pattern of living was composed in the oldest part of the city, where layer upon layer of time has sifted down, where rickety tenements rise on the ruins of a Caliphal palace, or rubbish dump.

[1] Their names mean *The Pyramids*, *The News* and *The Republic*. *Al-Ahram*, the oldest, was founded by the Takla brothers, two migrants from Lebanon, in 1875. A decree of 1960 abolished the private ownership of the press.

Writers about *baladi* Cairo a century ago—the most precise was
Edward Lane, author of *The Manners and Customs of the Modern
Egyptians*—described an ample city, if not an empty one. In 1836
a soaring population had not yet divided and subdivided the large
Arab houses with their cool internal courtyards, bringing untidi-
ness as well as congestion. When Stanley Lane Poole published
his description of Cairo seventy years later it was still possible to
expatiate thus on the ancient quarters:

After the bustle of the street this quiet and ample space is very
refreshing, and one feels that the Egyptian architects have happily
realized the requirements of Eastern life. They make the streets narrow
and overshadow them with projecting *meshrebiyas*, because the sun
beats down too fiercely for the wide streets of European towns to be
endurable. But they make the houses themselves spacious and surround
them with courts and gardens, because without air the heat of the
rooms in summer would be intolerable. The Eastern architect's art lies
in so constructing your house that you cannot look into your neigh-
bour's windows, nor he into yours; and the obvious way of attaining
this end is to build the rooms round a high court, and closely veil the
windows with lattice blinds, which admit a subdued light and sufficient
air, and permit an outlook without allowing the passing stranger to see
through. The wooden screens and secluded court are necessary to fulfil
the requirements of the Mohammedan system of separating the sexes.

Houses such as these are now museum pieces; [1] the separation
of the sexes is no longer an absolute requirement of Egyptian life.
This change is due in part to the modernist influence of such
thinkers as Muhammad Abdu, the rector of Cairo's Al-Azhar
University, who died the year before the book just quoted from
was published. As a result of the permeation of his ideas, with the
rethinking of the Muslim religion in terms of the twentieth
century, thousands of Cairo women work alongside men, not only

[1] For example, two houses adjoining Ibn-Tulun Mosque were maintained
in a largely seventeenth-century style by an English officer who has given his
name to what is now 'The Gayer-Anderson Museum'. In the old city two
remarkable Mameluke houses—those of Gamal al-Din al-Dhahabi and the
Sheikh al-Saheimi—are also maintained in a state that is no longer typical of
Cairo living (*see* map, pages 34–5).

in education but also in industry and administration. In Al-Azhar itself there are now women students of divinity.

Parallel to the modernization of Islamic thinking has been the consistent development, over a century, of a lay educational system, symbolized in Cairo by its two secular universities—to say nothing of the American University. Many of the younger writers and thinkers are convincedly secular; some are anti-clerical.

But even more than ideology, physical crowding makes the segregation of women unfeasible. The *harim* system never existed in the country, where unveiled women helped their menfolk in the fields. The *harim* was a luxury practised in cities. Burgeoning Cairo makes the *harim* impossible. For it is impossible to exaggerate the sheer animal growth of this largest city in Africa. It is not only that the Cairenes beget and re-beget; Cairo, like other capitals, has acted as a sponge, drawing hundreds of thousands of immigrants from the villages. The standard of living in Cairo has risen more rapidly than in the country. As a result every train from the south or the north brings new citizens to the centre. Cairo's population in 1882 was 374,838. In 1964 it was estimated at almost ten times that figure: it will pass four million by the time this book is a year old.

Old Cairo—the area within *muezzin*-call of the Citadel's mosques—is no longer the largest concentration of this traditional living. Shubra was the country village where Muhammad Ali built a rural palace. In 1896 it was still recommended in guide-books for those who wished to make an afternoon drive among the canals and buffaloes of the Egyptian countryside. To find countryside you must now go in other directions—west to the Pyramids, or south beyond Helwan. Shubra itself is a borough more congested than East Ham or Harlem. Hundreds of new streets have been colonized by the *baladi* way of life. If no longer rural, Shubra is worth visiting for the church of St Theresa of Lisieux, one of the most remarkable shrines anywhere. Originally started by an Anglo-Irish Carmelite in the twenties, a small chapel drew increasing crowds of Muslims as well as Christians. The huge new church is constantly visited by Egyptian mothers; they press their children, or articles of clothing, against the glass box in which lies the image of the saint. The entrance to the church is walled with *ex voto* tablets in more than a dozen languages; one is from a former Muslim prime minister of Egypt.

Abbasia is another quarter where the old city has burst its bounds, reaching into the plain that stretches to Heliopolis and the airport. The country palace of Habib Sakakini—a Gothic wonder with plump, 'ninetyish' caryatids and floriate scrolls inscribed with the Levantine pasha's intitials—is now the centre of a cross-roads of congested tenements. Even in the back-streets of Heliopolis (whose Arabic nickname, *Masr Gadida*, means 'New Cairo') the old ways reproduce themselves, absorbing transistors and washing-machines as a bird's nest may absorb ribbon or tinfoil. Radios blare from coffee-shops; people wear pyjamas in the street; forty thousand carts slow up the traffic; policemen in black uniforms (or white in summer) dispute with pedestrians so loudly that an innocent passer-by might expect a revolution—till all dissolves to the swift teeth-showing and respectful gestures of the East. Anger becomes the Muslim peace, or salaam. Here children teem like chicks, but chicks from no battery system: free-ranging, tumultuous, they are yet in awe of their fathers. Many are mischievous; some criminal: for these there are reformatories, if they are caught—and they are agile. Statistics, however, show little sign of that pointless delinquency which is sometimes a feature of more prosperous societies.

Cairo's *baladi* quarters are worth exploring. They are living survivals of the *Arabian Nights*. For though much of that greatest Arab novel was set in Baghdad, the society described is that of Cairo, and the way of life in many respects has not changed. The only way to explore is on foot. There is no danger—though you may have altercations if you produce a cold-eyed camera. This can cause indignation, a sense that you have abandoned the role of guest (so sacred to Arabs) for that of pryer, a butterfly-collector of customs, whose specimens of curious human behaviour will be exhibited to your friends at home in an atmosphere of mockery. For, tragically, these good-hearted people are beginning to feel that they are backward, that their vital lanes and open-air living may be, perhaps, degraded. Their own middle-class citizens have given them this idea more than outsiders. In truth, all that is best in Egypt comes from such lanes: a vitality hard to equal elsewhere, an enthusiasm and energy, which deserve admiration, for the little spontaneous important pleasures.

Not all middle-class Egyptians despise this way of living. The novelist Naguib Mahfouz has carefully documented it in a trilogy called *Between the Two Palaces*, a saga of *baladi* life recorded to the last detail. Yusif Shaheen, the most remarkable director of the Egyptian cinema, made a film about a schizophrenic in *gallabya* and set all the action in the noisy purlieus of Bab al-Hadid, Cairo's main rail terminus.

Chapter 5

Frangi

YET most *baladi* Cairenes, when they can afford them, buy trousers and adopt with them the *frangi* way of life. '*Frangi*' is antonym for '*baladi*'. It derives from the Arabic word for 'Frank', but designates all that is non-Egyptian and foreign. *Frangi* originally describes (besides trousers) dance music, cocktails, oil-paintings in drawing-rooms (instead of calligraphic texts), Louis Quinze furniture (reproduced for *frangi* clients by *baladi* carpenters), to say nothing of a bank account instead of a brassbound chest. *Originally*—these things are now so much part of the Cairo landscape that they are hardly felt as foreign any more.

The *frangi* Cairene, who nine times out of ten is a Muslim, must be distinguished from a '*Khawaga*', a noun properly used to denote a foreign Christian, though sometimes extended to Copts, the Egyptian Christians, as well. The *frangi* Muslim and the *Khawaga* will live side by side, more harmoniously than Christian and Muslim in Cyprus, but with reservations about each other. Their way of life is the same, but the once-potent *Khawaga* (who benefited when the Christian West directed Arab destinies) is now diminished. The term '*Khawaga*' itself (complimentary in Lebanon) carries in Cairo undertones of disrespect, so that one prefers to be addressed as '*Sayyid*', the current term for 'mister'.

The middle class is the ruling element in modern Cairo. From its ranks rise the makers of the city as it is today, the formers of its taste, the founders of its revolution. The middle class has recently risen from the *baladi* mass; the nineteenth century was well advanced before ordinary Egyptians were allowed to own land at

17

all, and it was from the breaking of the royal monopoly on land
that the bourgeoisie derives. Class barriers are fluid and the
middle class is growing. Two statistics hint its size: while only
seventy thousand people in Cairo have driving licences, six
hundred thousand are officially classed as government officials or
employees. The second category comprises those with at least one
foot on the middle-class ladder.

The middle class lives a little everywhere. From streets which
seem purely *baladi*—noisy with stalls and footballing children—
soar the nesting-blocks of *frangi* families. (These families themselves have *baladi* cousins back in the village or in some poorer
quarter of the city.) Some areas are almost entirely *frangi*. The
most prosperous and characterless is Zamalek, the northern mile
and a half of the Gezira island. Here bougainvillea, jacaranda and
poinsettia take it in turns to decorate roads where foreign
ambassadors and Egyptian notables have their houses. The
southern Gezira is dominated, physically by the Tower of Cairo
and socially by the Gezira Club, once the preserve of British
administrators and business men, now of their Egyptian inheritors.
Roda, the southern island, is a quarter of a mile shorter than the
Gezira. It is also less grand. Yet its close-packed blocks are
mostly approached by trousered legs, those in *gallabya* belonging
to servants or vendors. Roda's western shore is luxurious.

In one riverside palace the Greek wife of an Egyptian pasha had
three laboratories dedicated to Pharaonic medicine. On one
occasion a rich friend of hers, dying of ennui, longing to believe
in something, if only Evil, challenged her to use her powers, if
only to make him ill. She enclosed a tarantula in a jar with a mud
statue of the scoffer, embodying his hair and nail-parings.
Nothing happened. The mage had to go to Switzerland on urgent
business. When there she received a telegram: her friend was in
hospital, apparently dying of intestinal cancer. By telephone from
Zürich she conducted a rescue operation. Her servants broke into
her laboratory. In the jar they found that the tarantula, dying of

hunger, had bitten deep into the intestines of the statue, perhaps seeking the fragments of nail. The mage told her Nubian servants to wash the statuette in Nile water by moonlight. (The moon was fortunately large.) The victim at once recovered.

The west-bank governorate of Giza is also middle class. It surrounds a factory of middle-class values, the university. Middle class are the suburbs of Heliopolis and Maadi, once European, now increasingly Egyptian.

Few people are enthusiastic about the middle-class Egyptians. They aren't themselves. Every middle-class Cairene will join you in denouncing bourgeois values. There is something patronizing, anyway, in collective enthusiasms. 'I love pekes' from one voice is hardly different from another's 'I love Negroes'. The middle class in Cairo, as elsewhere, produces individuals. This is its justification. The characters in Fathy Ghanem's Cairo quartet, *The Man Who Lost His Shadow*, are, in the novelist's words, collectively ridiculous, cruel and tragic. But they are typical of the twentieth century everywhere: and lucky would be the Western reader who saw nothing of himself in the opportunist who is Ghanem's unheroic hero. This Cairo novel—with other Egyptian writing—shows the predicament of a class that has discarded the values as well as the costumes of the past. Ghanem has described an incident he remembers as important. His father, a villager, the first member of his family to discard the *gallabya*, went to a doctor to have the tattoo marks on his hands burnt off. The young boy had admired his father's tattoos and was sad to see the snakes and circles go. Older, he realized that this needless operation was a tragic symbol of a class that had abandoned a traditional scale of values for a new one it hardly comprehended.

Yet, for good or bad, middle-class aspirations shape the new city. Middle-class tastes dictate what is to be pulled down, what is to be built and what is to remain. The middle class celebrated its victory over the old regime by creating the twenty-five mile *corniche* along the Nile; a project which had been discussed for decades was created in a matter of weeks; Cairenes of all classes now enjoy what is virtually a new lung.

The middle class is impressed by size, modernity and comfort. The thirty-storey television building picked out in blue mosaic diffuses an image of middle-class living to those who own sets— or who stand round the screens put up in public places. Three channels provided, in 1964, 137 hours 16 minutes of weekly entertainment and instruction.

Middle class is the tower on the Gezira. Described in a government brochure as a masterpiece of neo-Islamic architecture, it resembles an immensely elongated waste-paper-basket. There is a roof restaurant which slowly revolves on itself, trundling slightly like a very slow train. Animated diners look up from their *escalope viennoise* to see that the panorama has totally altered: the Pyramids are on the fork side where, during the soup, the Citadel at least seemed constant.

Flute-seller in a Ramadan night

The great
mosque of
Al-Hakim:
one of the two
minarets,
' slender, vas
and intricate
(*page 52*)
◁

The oldest
mosque in
Cairo, that of
Amr Ibn al-
As (*page 43*)
▷

The mosque of
Ahmed Ibn Tulun:
the ablution
fountain and
limestone minaret
(*page 44*) ▷

The Citadel: Muhammad Ali's mosque (*page 30*) and the Mokattam hills

△ Cairo roofscape: Sultan Hassan's mosque at left (*page 54*), the Citadel at right

▽ Modern Cairo. *Left to right :* Arab League, the Nile Hilton, Municipality Building, River Nile behind

△ Three generations in a family glass factory

▽ Students prepare a wall newspaper

Feshawy café: Cairo's St Germain des Prés

**Bairam in Cairo: feluccas laden with holiday-makers,
the Hilton behind**

Chapter 6

Aristocratic

FIFTEEN years ago the middle class had none of the bounce and few of the luxurious apartments of today. Then there was an aristocracy to be in awe of, to set the tone. Since 1952 most of the aristocrats—and plutocrats—have gone abroad. Turkey has been favoured by those with Turkish blood but not too closely connected to the dispossessed Ottoman royalty. Others have chosen Switzerland, France, or (in the person of ex-King Farouk) Monte Carlo. Some linger on as unobtrusively as possible, on modest pensions (if they are former princes or princesses) or on what they have saved from nationalization and sequestration. They often retain the use of their furniture in beautiful palaces on miniscule incomes. One *grande dame* contrives exquisite jewellery from fragments of Fatimid glass or Coptic bonework obtained from antique-shops and antiquaries; her work is a glowing rebuke to the mass-produced tourist ware: it is sold for the benefit of Coptic charities. A prince plays Chopin at small receptions, again for charity. Many of the aristocrats who stay cannot envisage leaving Egypt. They are loyal to it with a passion which those who have supplanted them cannot always comprehend.

In Garden City live wealthy Copts, many of whom bought English books and affected a British way of life. It is astonishing —and a little sad—to visit them now in some book-lined study, to be asked hypnotically about some once fashionable name in London letters, about some 'Ted' or 'Malcolm', a proconsul or ambassador fallen into a footnote.

The Copts have abandoned English names. 'William', 'Geoffrey' or 'Cecil' have yielded to a discreeter 'Towfik', or even 'Gamal': ambiguous labels, possible for Muslim and Christian alike.

Chapter 7

Nubian

THE Nubians are another undominant class, though their antiquities are the preoccupation of tourists, their good looks the obsession of photographers and artists.

The Nubians are not found in any particular streets, but they share with new arrivals from the villages a quarter which would escape the notice of a casual boarder at the Hilton or Shepheard's. I myself first became aware of this strange quarter when staying at a pension on the thirteenth floor of a sub-skyscraper. It was early in the morning. I was awakened by cock-crow and then baa-ing. Looking down from my balcony I saw a village scattered on the flat roofs of the nearby buildings: six-storey tenements with a good deal of *art nouveau* ironwork and plaster decoration, the Oxford Street of Cairo. Ducks were quacking, sheep were chewing bales of clover and black-garbed women were pushing their hands into chicken coops for their children's breakfast. (Cairo eggs seem laid by pullets; you need at least four for an omelette.) In such roof-villages live the *bawabs*, or doormen, who are a feature of Cairo houses. For at the entrance to every tenement you see at least one sitting—more often, since they are sociable, a bench of them—eyeing who goes in and who comes out. The Nubians come from the narrow valleys between Aswan and the north Sudan; their villages are long, the Nile their high street; their houses are large, clean and airy, the white walls covered with pictures painted by the Nubians. Their houses have no locks, as theft is unknown—so, too, is adultery. The Cairenes say that it is because the Nubians are entirely honest that they are

23

employed as doormen. But nevertheless the Sudanese Government has protested to Egyptian producers that in their films dark people are always shown as servants, never as bosses.

Cairo is a city of great tolerance. And though friction may sometimes arise between *Khawaga* and Muslim, between wheat-coloured Egyptian and swarthy, there is no race prejudice as such, and if some lanes of Cairo resemble Harlem, it is a Harlem without complexes. If the Sudanese congregate in special cafés, it is not through segregation but preference. Every town and big village in the Nile valley has one particular Cairo café where its sons in exile congregate.

Sons—not daughters: Cairo's six thousand *baladi* cafés are still for men only.

Chapter 8

Necropolitan

ONE terminal quarter houses the majority—the dead.

A city, a *faubourg*, stretches in an arc parallel to the Cairo of the living, between its busy streets and the bare hills of Mokattam. This is the geometric street-plan you look down into if you stand by the Giyushi Mosque, above the Citadel, above the fort from which Napoleon shelled the rebellious city. It is not a graveyard, though graves are part of it. It is a lion-coloured, unlofty city, with streets like streets elsewhere, with the houses numbered, as though the postman might bring letters by the first delivery. But if he bangs the door and, no one opening, pushes in, he enters the parody of an ordinary house—two adjoining rooms, dust-carpeted, in each an oblong shape of stone or plaster. Under one floor lie the male members of the family; segregated in death, in the adjoining cellar are the women. The dead lie on slabs, shrouded, uncoffined. Visitable are the tombs of Mamelukes, Cairo's rulers for six centuries. Visitable, too, is the ornater nineteenth-century tomb-mosque of Muhammad Ali's descendants.

Visited recently was the tomb-house of his family by a young Egyptian born and brought up in America. An aunt was being buried. Still new to his own country, he was perplexed when a male relative approached him gravely, and said solemnly: 'I have just saluted your sister.' Then the young man remembered: there had been a sister, before his birth, who had died an infant. All these years she had been lying here, visitable.

To those who deny continuity between the Cairenes of today and the citizens of Memphis four thousand years ago, this *faubourg* is one answer. The Romans burned their dead; the Greeks buried them outside the city, by the roadside; early Islam recommended the simplest grave—one you could rub away with your hand. (The grave of King Ibn Saud in Riyadh is no longer remembered or visited, though he died but ten years ago.) No other Muslim capital has this burial system, or its concomitants. For at each key-point of the Cairo year—the feast that marks the end of Ramadan fasting, the longer feast that marks the pilgrimage to Mecca—the people swarm out to the cemetery cities, carrying picnic baskets, eager to visit those members of the family who can no longer wear new clothes or 'smell the air'. There are two departures from the customs of the Pharaohs, who did similar things in their season. The dead are no longer embalmed, and the cemeteries are on the east bank, where the sun rises. Except during the reign of the heretical Akhnaton, the ancient Egyptians buried their dead—lavishly embalmed, or cheaply, depending on the family's circumstances—on the west bank, the realm of Osiris.

Grave-robbers were a persistent problem to the Pharaohs. The Pyramids, the deep shaft-graves, were all attempts to outwit them. Grave-robbers worry the Cairenes of today as they did their ancestors. Guardians patrol the necropolis; for them and their families there are even small shops selling tea and notebooks; some of the houses are inhabited by living people. But despite the presence of the guardians, and the *ghouls* with which the superstitious populate the cemetery darkness, most families gash the shrouds of their dead to make them valueless for looting.

Chapter 9

Macedonian

WHAT distinguishes Cairo from any other city in Africa—or for that matter Asia—is that it has been, since the early nineteenth century, the capital of something approaching a modern state. The phrase is not used flatteringly: 'a modern state' binds bad with good. But Cairo's thirty courts of justice with 650 judges and counsellors, its three prisons with 8,000 prisoners, its 65 hospitals with 13,032 beds, its more than 1,100 traffic police all reflect, not just a capital, but a capital on modern lines. As an instance of an Eastern society in creative and persistent collision with the West, Cairo is also unique. Istanbul (in Europe, by its foundation a Western city) is no competitor. For though a similar collision took place in nineteenth-century Constantinople, the result was defeat. Atatürk moved his new capital to a small town in Anatolia. No one (except in August when Alexandria becomes 'the second capital') has thought of abandoning Cairo.

In the century and a half between Napoleon and Nasser one foreign family—so large that it is referred to by the august name of 'dynasty'—controlled the country. The founder of this family's fortunes was a Macedonian Muslim from Cavalla in northern Greece. The founder of Alexandria, the glittering capital of Ptolemaic Egypt, had been a Macedonian; Muhammad Ali, also from Macedonia, revived Alexandria (shrunk to a fishing village of five thousand people) and made Cairo the capital of his virtual kingdom. He had come to Egypt as a vassal of the Ottoman Sultan, commanded to resist Napoleon. He turned his vassalship into an insolent fiction; he became a convinced admirer of Napoleon. The French revolutionary and his provincial disciple combined in savage surgery spread over two operations: the destruction of the Mamelukes. Napoleon conducted the first phase near the village of Imbaba (now absorbed into the fabric of greater Cairo, and the site of a balloon theatre). His musket-bearing soldiers defeated the gallant and heraldic barons who had ruled Egypt for six centuries. But those who survived the battle escaped to Upper Egypt and Sudan, thence to return to their fief, so they thought, once Napoleon had returned to Paris. But Muhammad Ali—in a sense the last and most successful of the Mamelukes—invited them to a reception in the Citadel and there massacred them. The site can still be seen: the narrow defile leading to the Bab al-Azab. A favourite myth for nineteenth-century painters was the escape of Hassan Bey, who jumped his horse sheer over the terrace. In truth, Hassan Bey escaped through being too ill to accept the invitation. Other Mamelukes in the provinces were summarily murdered.

Who *were* the Mamelukes?

Their name in Arabic is a past participle passive, meaning 'the owned'. They were originally white slaves, imported to guard the caliphs who owned them. Just as in the Roman Empire the praetorian guards had soon controlled the emperor they pro-tected, deposing him when they wished and appointing his successor, so the mercenary bodyguards overruled the caliphs. These white slaves came from the north-eastern fringes of the Islamic world, in particular from the Caucasus and Turkistan. They were energetic, sometimes deeply pious, sometimes cynical, but never Egyptian. The chief Mameluke was the sultan. Suc-cession sometimes passed from father to son. A more usual pattern was for a ruling sultan to adopt a particular favourite; for this favourite either to kill his patron or to avenge him (and seize his power) when some other Mameluke had done the killing. The Mameluke system can be dated from the reign of Saladin, a Kurd, in the twelfth century. He and his successors enforced a system similar to the feudal system of the West, though the Mamelukes' racial difference from their subjects—the patient *fellahin* of the Nile valley—made them even less concerned with democratic rights (the phrase is, of course, an anachronism) than were the barons of medieval France and England. When Egypt was defeated by the Ottoman Turks in 1517, when the last sultan, Tuman Bey, was crucified at the Gate of Zuweyla, it looked for a moment as though the Mamelukes were finished, wiped out by severer Tudors. But, overburdened by their sudden empire, the Ottomans found it convenient to milk Egypt through the Mamelukes, and the old caste continued to rule until the end of the eighteenth century, under the nominal overlordship of a Turkish official.

The Mamelukes left two legacies to Cairo: a scattering of blue and green eyes in swarthy faces, and a plethora of magnificent buildings. Schools, hospitals, above all mosques—whose chief feature were their own domed tombs (the spirit of Pharaonic Egypt, the obsession with a worthy dwelling for eternity, infected them too)—embellished the capital of a country whose population shrank from cight millions to two. The Cairo they bequeathed to Napoleon and his Macedonian disciple was a tiny fragment of the Cairo of today. The modern city owes its expansion to its present shape to the dynasty of Muhammad Ali. Nine-tenths of modern Cairo is post-Mameluke.

Muhammad Ali never felt himself an Egyptian, though his son, the austere soldier Ibrahim, felt an affinity with the dark-skinned Arabs similar, *mutatis mutandis*, to that of T. E. Lawrence. Muhammad Ali spoke Turkish, not Arabic, felt himself Ottoman, not Arab or even Macedonian. He had almost as many children as Ibn Saud. At the same time he admired the new civilization of the West and wanted to adopt every one of its appliances. He built steam-engines and lighthouses.

Muhammad Ali's impress on Cairo radiated from the Citadel.

Within ghost-shriek of the Bab al-Azab he built his palace, Al-Gawhara, 'The Jewel'; beside it, in his great mosque, is his tomb. To lovers of Islamic architecture this mosque is no more typical of the best in Cairo than the Opéra of the best in Paris. But the site of the mosque is magnificent, and though Turkish rather than Egyptian it dominates the eastern skyline.

Muhammad Ali linked Alexandria to Cairo by the Mahmoudia Canal. He founded the great barrage across the apex of the Delta; but, as with much of his work, the foundations were shaky and it was not completed till the nineties. A painting in the Gawhara Palace shows the reformer seated; so does Robert Curzon's description:

The Pasha at that time was a hale, broad-shouldered, broad-faced man; his nostrils were very much opened; and with his quick, sharp eye he looked like an old grey lion. We discoursed for three-quarters of an hour about the possibility of laying a railway across the Isthmus of Suez, which was the project then uppermost in the Pasha's mind; but the circumstance which most strongly recalls this audience to my memory, and which struck me as an instance of manners differing entirely from our own, was, in itself, a very trivial one. The Pasha wanted his pocket handkerchief, and looked about and felt in his pocket for it, but could not find it, making various exclamations during his search, which at last were answered by an attendant from the lower end of the room. 'Feel in the other pocket,' said the servant. 'Well, it is not there,' said the Pasha. 'Look in the other, then.' 'I have not got a handkerchief,' or words to that effect, were replied to immediately: 'Yes, you have.' 'No, I have not.' 'Yes, you have.' Eventually this attendant, advancing up to the Pasha, felt in the pocket of his jacket, but the handkerchief was not to be found; then he poked all round the Pasha's waist, to see whether it was tucked into his shawl; that would not do. So he took hold of his Sovereign and pushed him half over on the divan, and looked under him to see whether he was sitting on the handkerchief; then he pushed him over on the other side. During all these manœuvres the Pasha sat as quietly and passively as possible. The servant then, thrusting his arm up to the elbow in one of the pockets of his Highness's voluminous trousers, pulled out a snuff-box, a rosary and several other things, which he laid upon the divan. That would not

do either; so he came over to the other pocket, and diving to a pro-
digious depth he produced the missing handkerchief from the recesses
thereof, and with great respect and gravity, thrusting it into the
Pasha's hand, he retired again to his place at the lower end of the hall.

This description is worth repeating when we survey the
impress which the great man made on his captured capital and
when we hear the attacks of modern nationalists. Ruthless and
opportunist he may have been; his reforms were premature,
shallow and inspired by the wrong motives (he wanted to make
Egypt the base of an empire for himself); yet no one with these
easy, informal manners could fail to charm the Egyptians. To this
day, in all Arab countries, such ease of manner facilitates the
successful ruler. Muhammad Ali's successors lacked his genius
and relatedness to the East. His name was ill-commemorated in
Cairo. 'It was Ismail, under French influence, who made that
unspeakable atrocity, the "Boulevard Muhammad Ali", which
cut through one of the most beautiful quarters, ruined palaces and
gardens, and chopped off half of a noble mosque, in order to
preserve the tasteless accuracy of its straight line.' So Stanley Lane
Poole. At least Ismail's atrocity had arcades, giving it the air of an
oriental Rue de Rivoli. To Ismail's grandson, Farouk, the oriental
atmosphere seemed backward; the arcades were patchily removed.
Renamed Shari al-Qala (Citadel Street), it is one of the ugliest
thoroughfares in a beautiful city.

The Cairenes—tired of being ruled by Muhammad Ali's
descendants—have been taking their revenge on the monuments
of the dynasty.

Abdin Palace, in restrained Buckinghamesque style, faces a great
square. Here Ismail's son, Towfik, clashed in a dramatic argu-
ment with Colonel Arabi, the proto-Nasser of the eighties. The
great square, renamed Midan Gumhouriya, is turned into a gaudy
tent each July when the anniversary of the 1952 revolution is
commemorated by a speech to thousands. The palace itself is in
part a ministry (for land reform), in part a youth club and in part

a museum. Most of the elegant furniture was sold; what remains shows the taste of Ismail, whose Civil List was larger than Queen Victoria's, and whose wives hang in oils, dressed like Oxford landladies. In the royal bathroom the medicaments are as they were when King Farouk abdicated; the scales are a sad reminder of a weight that waxed as a reputation waned.

The palace where Ismail entertained the Empress Eugénie of France is on the east side of the Gezira. It was for long the town house of a rich Upper Egyptian Coptic family, the Lutfullahs. It is now the Omar al-Khayyam Hotel, preserved more or less as it was but surrounded by expensive chalets in the grounds.

The palace of Prince Muhammad Ali (Farouk's heir until his second queen, Narriman Sadik, presented him with a son shortly before his fall) still stands on Roda Island. Behind massive walls a cactus walk and an avenue of *banian* trees are unforgettable; both would do excellently for a surrealist film, if such were made in Egypt. The prince's palace has an impressive collection of royal and presidential photographs, conventionally autographed. The fake-Eastern *décor* of Damascus inspiration changes in the lavatory to Edwardian porcelain flowers. The prince built a museum in the grounds. It is an excellent place to inspect oriental carpets, royal portraits, illuminated Korans and other valued objects of an Eastern potentate with cautious good taste.

The paragraph as I have written it remains unchanged. But already, with the speed which characterizes change in the new East, it is out of date. A neon sign now hangs outside the palace, renamed 'Manyal Omar al-Khayyam'. It, too, is an hotel; its gardens are chalet-broken. The film would no more be *L'Année Dernière à Manyal*; the *banians* and the cactuses are tamed by tourists—by you and me in indigestible quantities—and the magic vanishes at the touch of hard currency.

No Cairo Betjeman protests at the degradation or demolition of the nineteenth century. This is sad, but understandable. For all its ugliness, the Victorian Age was one of power to Englishmen; to

Egyptians the age of Ismail and Towfik was one of humiliation. Ibrahim Pasha, a great general, retains a measure of respect; he retains too his statue, nobly equestrian, outside the Opera. But Suliman Pasha, the Frenchman who embraced Islam and was, among other things, the ancestor of Farouk's mother, lasted in his baggy trousers and fez only until 1964. Then he was removed from the square near Groppi's, where for decades he had turned his back on fat women making bee-lines for chocolates. His replacement?—a squat likeness of Talaat Harb, the founder of Bank Masr.

For those with a taste for the recent past, nowhere is more rewarding—while it still stands—than the Cairo Railway Museum. Tucked away near Bab al-Hadid it houses a wealth of models and photographs. They bear witness to Egypt's early entry to the age of railways. Muhammad Ali had discussed a railway with Curzon; one was opened from Alexandria to Cairo in 1856. In a special shed is preserved the 'kiosk engine' of Said Pasha, the ruler who authorized the building of the Suez Canal. This Rolls-Royce of a train was built by Messrs R. Stephenson and delivered in 1862. The painted exterior is as elaborate as the Bohemian glass made specially for Eastern patrons; the interior a curious mingling of stuffed upholstery and polished machinery. Said Pasha—the most obese of a never slim dynasty—reputedly drove this engine himself on visits to the estates of his relatives and friends.

Ismail was *par excellence* the builder of modern Cairo. To him the new quarters owed whatever they had of Italianate grace, sometimes elegance; for him was named the vast square once frowned on by a British barracks, now made gaudy by the Hilton. A brawn-red plinth is the square's umbilical; tenantless, for portly Ismail in his fez and frock-coat will never climb it. The square, no longer Ismailia, is Midan al-Tahrir—the last word meaning 'liberation'.

The jewel of Ismail remains the Opera. Rushed up from wood and plaster for the opening of the Suez Canal, its speed of Eastern

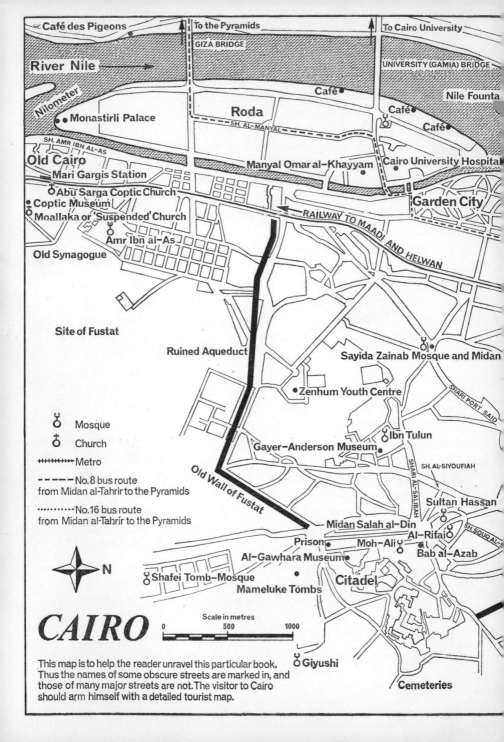

Café des Pigeons

To the Pyramids
GIZA BRIDGE

To Cairo University

River Nile

UNIVERSITY (GAMIA) BRIDGE

Nilometer

Café

Nile Founta

Roda

Café

Monastirli Palace

SH. AL-MANYAL

Café

SH. AMR IBN AL-AS

Old Cairo

Manyal Omar al-Khayyam

Cairo University Hospital

Mari Gargis Station

Abu Sarga Coptic Church

Garden City

Coptic Museum

Moallaka or 'Suspended' Church

RAILWAY TO MAADI

Amr Ibn al-As

AND HELWAN

Old Synagogue

Site of Fustat

Ruined Aqueduct

Sayida Zainab Mosque and Midan

SHARI PORT SAID

Zenhum Youth Centre

Mosque

Ibn Tulun

Church

SH. AL-SIYOUFIAH

Metro

Gayer–Anderson Museum

No.8 bus route
from Midan al-Tahrir to the Pyramids

Old Wall of Fustat

Sultan Hassan

No.16 bus route
from Midan al-Tahrir to the Pyramids

Midan Salah al-Din

Al-Rifai

Prison

Moh-Ali

Bab al-Azab

N

Al-Gawhara Museum

Shafei Tomb–Mosque

Citadel

Mameluke Tombs

CAIRO

Scale in metres
0   500   1000

Giyushi

This map is to help the reader unravel this particular book.
Thus the names of some obscure streets are marked in, and
those of many major streets are not. The visitor to Cairo
should arm himself with a detailed tourist map.

Cemeteries

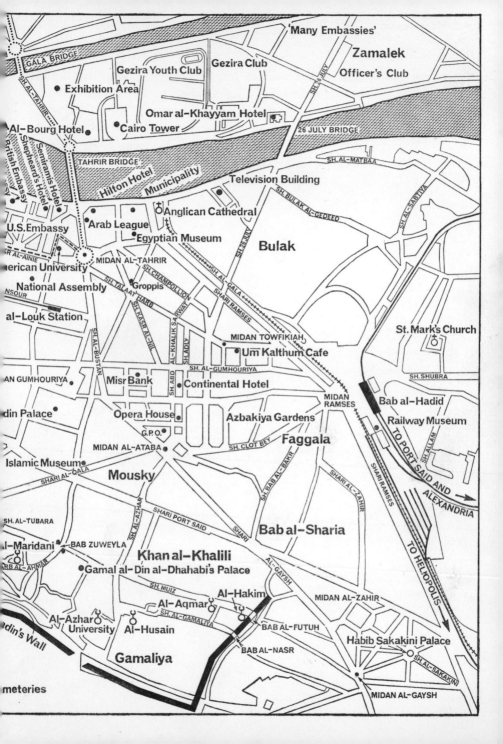

building was not matched by the commissioned composer. Verdi's *Aida* was not ready; *Rigoletto* was performed instead. On 28th April 1964 I saw an excellent performance of *La Traviata*—in Arabic. The translation by Ibrahim Rifaat was eminently singable; but the ladies of Violetta's *salon* came from a more democratic age than Ismail's, whose initial 'I' remains entangled in the wrought iron and gilt of the Opera's doorway.

Chapter 10

Exotic

BEHIND the dynasty, or in collusion with it, foreigners made much of (and from) the city.

Baron Herz deserved well of art lovers for being the dynamo of a committee for the preservation of Islamic buildings. But for him—to cite one example from dozens—the intricate wooden screen in Al-Maridani's mosque would have crumbled to dust.

Another baron, Empain, a Belgian, was the moving spirit in the development of Heliopolis: Cairo's northern suburb, founded in 1906, now has a population of 122,000. From profits made on trams Empain erected one of the city's most curious structures— the Hindu Palace. Externally it is an exact replica of one of the temples of Madura—gingerbread tower, elephantine statues, grotesque gargoyles—yet inside the baron furnished his residence with middle-class Belgian chairs and sofas, to say nothing of net curtains.

Empain was the kind of foreign adventurer for whom the pre-revolutionary economy was a rich pasture. He was not, of course, popular. His Regency manners did not fit with the courtly East. He was a brawler. But he enjoyed the friendship of King Fuad (Farouk's father) and royal favour paid off in economic concessions.

Another king presided at one of Empain's few defeats. On the Riviera in the twenties Empain had been presented to the still reigning Alfonso XIII of Spain. Later Alfonso paid a visit to Egypt in the strictest incognito. The baron invited him to dinner

D   37

at the Hindu Palace. The king accepted. When he passed the gargoyles, however, it was to find that the other guests were gamblers, night-club cronies of the baron, and cabaret performers. The Spanish king sat down to dinner. Sitting was his only action. He did not eat, did not drink, did not speak. Five minutes of this silent guest reduced the company to rocks. When the meal was over the king got up and, still silent, left.

Since the revolution the Hindu Palace has been left unused, a brown elephant in a scabrous garden whose palms have died, since no one has paid the water bills. At one time a Saudi Arabian prince proposed turning it into a rest-house for fellow Saudis in need of Egyptian air. The project fell down when the municipal authorities discovered the kind of rest-house that was intended.

More decorous survivors of foreign influence: the restaurants and hotels with English names. At the St James restaurant—where giant Red Sea prawns are a speciality—the proprietor proudly shows a cutting that brings back the past: it is from the *Egyptian Gazette* of 1895:

> Next season the new rooms will be furnished as bachelor quarters where gentlemen will find bedrooms with breakfasts on the system similar to that in London in the neighbourhood of the West-End clubs.

Except for its name, which goes back to the times when an enterprising Victorian founded a hostelry for those who shortened the voyage to India by disembarking at Alexandria and taking the train to Suez, Shepheard's today has little that is Anglo-Saxon. The old Shepheard's was an island of English imperial living. Old newspapers evoke what went on amidst the bamboo furniture and potted palms. New Year's Day 1915, for example. In the 'Egyptian Hall' the dancers in fancy dress waltzed and lancered. Then at midnight:

A sudden whirring brought some of the assembled guests back to earth as a realistic model of an aeroplane rose gracefully from the hall to the topmost point of the ballroom. Seated in it was a pretty child, with gauzy wings, his little face wreathed in a happy smile to the assembly. Doves were released, bearing streamers with messages of good will, and snowballs were flung by all—soft souvenirs—not so soft, alas, for the young subaltern whose snowball flew into the hall and struck General Maclaren in the face: a sticky moment, soon resolved by an affable word from the General. At last it was all over and Cairo went home, bewildered, weary—and happy.

Other foreign influences contributed to that Cairo. French (despite the virtual British protectorate) was spoken more than English. A cultural influence remains, diluted by decree. There is a Lycée, the Jesuits still have their college and the Institut d'Egypte is an indirect descendant of the institute founded by Napoleon. The American University at Cairo is even expanding; its students act *The Glass Menagerie*.

And scattered all over the city in discreet bed-sitting rooms are foreigners from Central Europe like my friend Yanko. He is a Slovak aristocrat, who paints. He lives in an apartment overlooking the Ministry of Religious Endowments. He wears dark glasses, stays with his books and cactuses, drinks *zebeeb* on a balcony that looks on to the crowd. He goes out only to buy vegetables in the Bab al-Louk covered market or more *zebeeb* from the Greek grocer on the corner. He also attends the dozens of art exhibitions which are a feature of Cairo's life. His own pictures— he has just done a series of 'Juvenile Delinquents' in wash on crumpled paper—hang in the Salon d'Automne.

'Cairo painting? A few genuine islands in a sea of epigonism.' I raise an eyebrow in incomprehension.

'Epigonism? My word: decadent imitation, like the late Greek rulers of Alexandria. Not surprising. Prince Yusif Kemal opened the Fine Arts Academy in 1908. Most of the teachers were French. What is surprising is that after fourteen centuries' break in representational art—the Fatimids a brief exception—the Egyptians are returning to painting with such enthusiasm. Khadeega Riad, grand-daughter of the poet Ahmed Showky, exhibits abstract paintings. I prefer her jewellery—it is superb. Raouf Abdul Mageed turns beach-huts into abstract patterns: a sinister, silent, private universe. I like best Effat Nagi. Her brother Muhammad was famous for his pictures of Haile Selassie which he painted in Abyssinia before the Italian war. Effat restores magic—always a part of Egypt—real magic, sinister magic, not "glamour"—to painting. She disregards good taste and fashion—those two quicksands. Her magic symbols in fretwork relief—three-dimensional—glisten with fluorescent paint.'

Yanko has taken to photography. He stayed up all night to photograph one brief-lived cactus which blossoms every three years. 'Flowers,' Yanko says a little bitterly; 'Yes, Cairo is full of flower-shops. To the Cairenes, though, they're things you put in a silver basket, with ten yards of ribbon, and send to a wedding.'

Once again what I write is overtaken by events. I have just had a postcard from Yanko. It was postmarked Munich.

Chapter 11

Islamic

Its Islamic architecture makes Cairo a unique, not merely an important city. 'Islamic': because the nineteenth-century 'Saracenic' was always inaccurate and because, in the words of the greatest living authority, 'the term "Arab" should never be used to designate the architecture of Islam'.[1]

Cities other than Cairo have, perhaps, singly more perfect Islamic buildings—though even this is a question of debate. Everyone who has seen them admires the glowing colours of Bursa. Lovers of pure architectural form acclaim the hunting palace of Ukhaidir or the fragmentary palaces of ninth-century Samarra. The water-fronted Taj Mahal has as many admirers as photographers. But these are either single buildings or, in the case of Bursa, buildings of a single epoch. Only Cairo shows a constant development, century after century, from naïveté through simplicity to complication, through efflorescence to decadence, so that a whole culture manifesting itself in stone, brick and wood for more than thirteen centuries awaits the visitor. Baghdad might have rivalled Cairo. But Baghdad was ravaged by the Mongols only a few years after the completion of the delicately harmonious Mustansaria. If we are to appreciate Islamic art, 'uncorrupted by the mechanical detail of the Alhambra, unspoilt by the

---

[1] Professor Creswell himself uses the term 'Muslim'; but I may be excused for preferring the adjective derived from Islam, the name for the religion and its culture, rather than the participle describing one who has embraced Islam. One advantage of my term is that it fits buildings whose architects were Christian.

41

over-elaboration of Delhi, we must', in the words of Stanley
Lane Poole, 'study the mosques and tombs of Cairo'.

If Cairo—with the haphazard growth of its quarters—seems
complicated, its virtue is that looked at closely it unravels not
only its own complications but those of the half-alien, half-
familiar civilization at whose hub it stands. Unravelling, it
explains.

One long day's walk (though it might be wiser to spread the
episodes over several days) can lead to an instructive under-
standing of this civilization of the south-eastern Mediterranean
and its evolution.

The journey should begin at the south of the modern city. The
best way to start the journey: take a local train from Bab al-Louk
station. (The first-class fare is three piastres: about sixpence.)
Alighting at the third station, Mari Gargis, you enter a nearscape
of rather ugly churches. Saluting these, noting the two circular
bastions of the Roman city, but resolving to visit this Cairo
'tomorrow', you follow a sombre, dusty lane outside the Christian
enclave to the site of the earliest mosque in Egypt.

Egypt was conquered in 640-1, and the conqueror, Amr Ibn
al-As, was thus a young contemporary of his Prophet, who had
died in 632. Amr came from an Arabia in which, once more to
quote Professor Creswell, 'it would appear that the pre-Islamic
Arabs had but the crudest notions of buildings, that their principal
sanctuary before 608 was nothing more than four walls the height
of a man enclosing the sacred well Zemzem. . . . In other words,
Arabia constituted an almost perfect architectural vacuum'. Amr,
who had drunk the water of Zemzem, was a soldier of genius. He
was a simple believer in a simple faith and needed a place in which
to worship. He saw the originals of the churches we have just
passed; unlike the churches farther east in Syria and Palestine,
they are rather poky places, reflecting something internal, rather
tenebrous in the Coptic attitude to religion. I mention Syria and
Palestine because there the Muslims for a long time shared the

churches, taking one end for their prayers and leaving the other
to the Christians.

Today, where Amr faced his problem, we see a great brick wall,
plaster-covered, rather derelict. There are three entrances. Inside
we contemplate an empty space of earth and sand. This central
courtyard is known as the *sahn*, a technical term we might
remember. On the far side from the entrance we see the sanctuary,
a forest of assorted pillars opening on to the *sahn* through twenty
arches.

This vast mosque, bare, simple, was essentially a military
building, a place where an army of male believers could assemble
within protecting walls and get on with its devotions.

Only the ghost of the site frequents what we see today. Hardly
one brick or purloined pillar can remain from Amr's original
building, which was tiny in comparison with what we see today,
in keeping with the 'city of the tent', Fustat, which Amr improvised outside the Christian Babylon. As against the giant quad-
rangle of today (more than a hundred yards long on each side)
Amr's mosque was a rectangle measuring about 29 by 17 yards.
The floor was of earth strewn with pebbles. Palm-bole columns
supported a roof where palm leaves were thatched with mud as in
Muhammad's own house in Medina. The unplastered walls were
of mud brick.

Yet Amr's mosque—rebuilt thirty years later, again enlarged,
then allowed to collapse, then restored and restored again up to
the time of Muhammad Ali—is the right point of departure in a
tour of Islamic Cairo. As we come out and look for a taxi (they are
hard to find in this impoverished quarter) we are on the site of the
first Islamic Cairo, a city of tents assembled by nomads. The
modern scenery—mounds of rubbish, graveyards and stalls
selling crude pottery—seems right.

The movement of builders was always to the north.

The next City—that of a viceroy of the Abbasid caliph in Iraq
—was a mile north and two hundred years later than Fustat. Ibn

Tulun came to Egypt from Samarra. There the Caliph Mutassim
—tired of the frequent clashes between his Turkish mercenaries
and the Arabs of Baghdad—had built the first megalopolis since
ancient Rome: a city of sharp angles, vast boulevards whose almost
Brasilian planning is still visible in aerial photographs. Coming
from this large city, Ibn Tulun, himself a Turk, found Amr's city
confined while his people found the mosque of Amr, though
enlarged, too small for the purposes of Friday prayer. Nothing
compared with the Friday Mosque of Samarra, in which sixty
thousand people could say their prayers at once.

So in 870 Ibn Tulun proceeded to build a new city with a palace
for himself and a hippodrome for polo. (Turks and Arabs were
united on one thing—a love of horses.) But above all what united
Ibn Tulun to his subjects and made irrelevant the modern
obsession with 'nationality' was religious faith. Ibn Tulun was a
pious Muslim and it is his mosque, miraculously intact, which we
can visit today.

This great solemn square can be spoken of in the same breath
with the Parthenon. To my mind it is yet more numinous: though
like a Pharaonic rather than a Greek temple it conceals its beauty
behind outer walls which the worshipper must penetrate. The
mosque is set on a slight hill, secure from floods; but it is no
Acropolis. Turbulent crowded streets (rather uglily tidied up by
municipal planners) lead to its gates. Inside it is serene, simple,
composed of the elements. The *sahn*, open to the colourless sky, is
sunbleached, yellow; in the centre a domed ablution fountain (it
dates from 1296) is inferior to the original whose dome was up-
held by ten marble columns and which was put there for aesthetic
purposes; we know this, since washing facilities were provided *en
masse* beyond the western wall. If the *sahn* stands for the desert, the
fountain for an oasis, the arcades are the forest of the soul's anti-
podes, cool, meditative, full of spiritual delight: a forest which
the Muslims who controlled the deserts of the Middle East had
briefly seen—the date groves of the Tigris, the cedar forests of

Mount Lebanon—and for their rarity had remembered, just as the Koran itself, revealed in the Meccan dust-bowl, becomes incandescent when it speaks of gardens. Sky, desert, water, forest, evoke the fifth element in which all have their being: God. For this is a building where God is not manifest in statues (there are, of course, none) or details (though the plaster window-grilles are exquisite) but in a total harmony, where nothing obtrudes but where each region of the soul can find its symbol.

Outside the great mosque, in the additional area between it and the high temple-walls, is a limestone minaret which resembles a misshapen *ziggurat*. Several theories try to account for this strange tower, half square, half helicoidal. According to one suggestion, Ibn Tulun was an irascible activist who detested idlers. When he was discussing his mosque—whose innovation would be its dispensing with the columns normally looted from churches—Ibn Tulun was seen playing with a piece of paper. Caught out in the idle gesture, he rationalized:

'Build me a minaret like this spiral!'

Another more plausible theory is that he remembered the great whirling spiral of the mosque in Samarra, itself part of an Iraqi landscape where in Ibn Tulun's day the *ziggurat* at Babylon still stood and where, to this day, the stump of Aga Guf rises to a height of 170 feet on the Baghdad skyline. Yet unlike the brick piers covered with plaster, unlike the decoration of the arcades and the grilles in the windows, the minaret is not the original, for it was almost certainly entirely rebuilt by Lajin in the Mameluke period. In its present shape it is perhaps a clumsy attempt, in an age when minarets had become graceful to the point of effeminacy, to restore an original which had used the fluid lines of Samarra's great spiral without confusion. In Ibn Tulun's time the minaret will not have seemed eccentric. The minaret—as an architectural form—was only starting on its centuries of evolution. The first minarets had been square towers round the great church in Damascus, converted to a mosque. The word 'minaret'

originally means 'a place of fire', and would have described a
lighthouse such as the great Pharos at Alexandria.

The next city—and the first to be called 'Cairo'—lies a mile
farther north of Ibn Tulun's mosque. It was born a century later.
Here no train or tram can help us. It would be wise to abandon
taxis and trust to legs—always provided that Amr's mosque was
visited at dawn and Ibn Tulun's near breakfast.

This third Islamic city has a southern gate, robust and Byzan-
tine, its two bastions surmounted by delicate later minarets, to
welcome us. (In the past it welcomed criminals, an arch of sighs.
After being a place of execution it became the secret abode of Al-
Mutawalli. The latter was an airborne saint who would levitate
from Mecca to Cairo as easily as a character in the *Arabian Nights*.
It is to him that the invocatory notes are written, pushed between
nails and the wood; for his pity the shreds of cloth.)

To get to this gate—its name in Arabic is 'Bab Zuweyla', except
to those who, remembering the saint, call it 'Bab al-Mutawalli'—
there are two easy roads from Ibn Tulun. Each is interesting. If
you walk idly, not pausing to examine any particular monument
but imbibing a general view of perfect and broken buildings,
either of the two roads gives an urban exuberance and vitality that
go with advancing day and contrast with the dawnlit tombs of
Amr's site and with Ibn Tulun's austere fundamentals. To find
these two roads any plan of the medieval monuments of Cairo will
be adequate; the map in this book should also be sufficient. The
two roads run roughly parallel to each other in a northward direction, the Nile to your left, the Citadel and its bare hills to your
right. Both roads start the same. You leave the mound of Ibn
Tulun and turn left, from the doorway, till you reach the Shari
al-Salibah. This street runs from the east to the west, descending
from the great *midan* below the Citadel as far as the square of
Sayida Zainab [1] and by extension to the Nile.

[1] Sayida Zainab, a daughter of the Prophet, is buried in a reconstructed
mosque in Cairo which non-Muslims should not attempt to visit.

Shari al-Salibah is itself a street to return to at night. A Turkish
fountain, an ancient bath with a waist-cloth across the doorway, a
twin-domed mosque, tomb of two Mameluke friends—nowhere
better before bedtime in a slow taxi. But now it is day and follow-
ing Shari al-Salibah towards the Citadel you come to a cross-
roads. A tea-shop (but dismiss any Western connotation) is placed
conveniently across from a *sebeel* (an enclosed fountain) con-
structed in such Turkish fantasy that Central Asia, not Africa,
seems for a moment our background: a partial dome, topped by a
crescent, five flanks visible of floridest Ottoman relief with
windows of intricate grille-work. Beside it a small stall offers
onions. It is watched over by a white-capped elder. At the table
next to mine in the tea-shop (I am repeating this walk with a stop-
watch for my readers) an old wizened man in a turban sips *'erfa*,
a milk charged with cinnamon.

The *sebeel* is a landmark. The first road to Bab Zuweyla begins
here. It is called, in its first stage, Shari al-Siyoufiah. The line of
the road runs straight through four name-changes. It crosses only
one large thoroughfare—the street once named after Muhammad
Ali, now after the Citadel: but you press on, taking care to avoid
the heavier traffic and to maintain the axis you have followed.
Except for this one collision with trams and buses our road is an
all but continuous market. Cadavers of buffalo meat, violet-
stained, hang against walls built before the potato (also on sale)
had been brought from America. Men make carpets in cubicle-
shoplets. I see, by chance, as I time this walk on an average May
morning, four chopped-off camel's feet waiting for buyers. A
little farther a barrow of glistening green peppers makes me want
to make a salad. Next to them giant tomatoes, not like our
Western billiard balls, but misshapen as Breughel's peasants. A
boy rushes past a shop that sells gold necklets. He waves a spray of
green stuff. He shouts: '*N'na'!*' which sounds impossible but
means 'mint'. A new aroma joins many. A wall is a pattern of
shoes, slippers, sandals. A woman in black hawks different pulses

—so complex that, unlike the peppers, they give me no temptation of the kitchen. A concrete shop, very ugly, is walled with packets of a well-known soap powder. I pause again where the road expands slightly into an oblong. There is a café with an awning, *baladi* but comfortable, belonging to 'Muhammad Nasif and his sons'. I drink the Nasifs' Turkish coffee (*sada*, that is, neat, without sugar) while a donkey pulls a dray of large jars, their mouths stopped with paper. The jars contain *ful mudammas*, the *fava* beans which, soaked in oil and seasoned, are the porridge of Cairo's breakfast tables. I pay for coffee—fivepence—and passing a display of children's chamber pots enter the road's last section, a covered *souq* (the word 'bazaar' belongs to India, not Egypt), far superior in interest to the more famous Khan al-Khalili, a tourist trap since the days of *Bella Donna*. This *souq* offers the nearest thing left to the daily life of Mameluke Cairo. Vast doors (they are now held open permanently) are studded with iron; the merchants used to shut them when the Mamelukes were rowdy. Here you can buy genuine mementoes of the East to do with four-legged beasts, for this *souq* devotes itself to the needs of horse and donkey. Saddles and saddle-cloths, woollen head-trappings, these things are decorative, reasonably priced and functional. And the *souq* with its pale filtered light leads abruptly to Bab Zuweyla.

I look at my watch: the walk from Ibn Tulun (with a break for tea at the *sebeel*, a break for coffee later) has taken me an hour precisely.

The other road, equally interesting, is longer and more winding. Go along Shari al-Siyoufiah and take the first turning on the right, as though up to the Citadel. Two vast mosques (one of which, Sultan Hassan, will be visited later) stand astride the roadway, looking down on to a plainlet. Do not approach the mosques, but cross the ugly Shari al-Qala and go down Shari Souq al-Silah— 'Street of the Arms Market'—a crumbling, congested alley of fragments. Follow it to its conclusion, bearing left into Shari

al-Tubara, which passes the mosque of Al-Maridani,[1] and turns into
the westward-circling Darb al-Ahmar. Mosques, ancient schools,
Eastern music, shops, cafés, once more the necessary atmosphere
to lead you abruptly to Bab Zuweyla, this time not facing you but
towering on your right.

I keep leading up to Bab Zuweyla as if this gateway were a
prima donna. She is: for she marks the entrance to the essential
Cairo.

For just as the essential London is a walled nucleus at the core
of a built-up wen, so the essential Cairo takes its name and nucleus
from a quadrilateral hardly more than a thousand paces on each
side. This inner city—built for religion and rule rather than for
ordinary living—was Al-Medina Al-Qahira, the Conquering City.
The geometrical shape (still discernible to the patient) is bounded
by its original walls in the north, the later wall of Saladin in the
east, Darb al-Ahmar and its continuation Taht al-Rabeh in the
south and the ghost of the Canal in the west.

This Cairo lasted in its true form for two centuries. We know
the precise date of its foundation: 5th May 969, the night after
Gawhar had conquered the streets of Amr and Ibn Tulun on
behalf of his master Al-Mo'izz. Gawhar was a Muslim slave of
European origin; his master was the fourth member of a Tunisian
Arab dynasty which laid claim to the caliphate as descendants of
the Prophet's daughter, Fatima.[2] Fatima had married Ali, the
cousin and enthusiastic disciple of Muhammad. A sect of Islam

---

[1] Al-Maridani's mosque, built in 1339, brilliantly illustrates the extra-
ordinary power of synthesis in Arabic-Islamic art. The pillars are of every
shape and size: red granite from Pharaonic temples; Greco-Roman; Coptic
Christian; capitals are gilt lotus or flowery Corinthian; several are even
upside down. Yet the way they have been used imposes a surprising unity,
a delicacy even, which is impressive. This ability to blend many disparate
elements in one new style is a distinctive feature of Arabic Islam. The
meshrebiya screen which separates the carpeted 'sanctuary' from the arcaded
courtyard is a remarkable, if much restored, example of fourteenth-century
woodwork. Al-Maridani, son-in-law and cup-bearer to the prolific Mameluke
ruler, Al-Nasir Muhammad, was later governor of Aleppo, where he died.
[2] All of the Prophet's male children died before puberty.

(the Shia) believed that the true spiritual headship of the Muslim community could pass only through descendants of Ali's marriage with Fatima. The Shia (who still comprise half the population of Iraq and nearly all the population of Persia) have been in a sense the Stuarts of Islam, while the Sunnis, the majority, have been the sensible Hanoverians. Egypt today is a Sunni country, but the nucleus of its capital was the Shia foundation we enter through Bab Zuweyla. On the northern side of the Fatimid quadrilateral is Bab al-Nasr. Over this more masculine gateway survives a Kufic inscription: to the 'No god but God and Muhammad is the Prophet of God' of all Muslims is added the phrase, 'and Ali is the deputy of God'.

The details of how Gawhar founded Cairo are curious. He mustered an army of diggers and lined them on the borders of the quadrilateral he had planned. The area was marked by stakes, on whose tops ran a light cord with bells. Moroccan astrologers stood ready with their quadrants and tables of reckoning. Only when they would pronounce the moment propitious would the rope be jerked and the primitive telephone set its bells ringing. In the event, a raven alighted on the cord and forestalled the star-wise. It was too late to stop the picks and shovels of the waiting thousands. The astrologers could only declare what planet had been in the ascendant in the moment of the raven's *faux pas*. It was the worst: the baleful red planet Mars. Its name in Arabic is 'Al-Qahir'—'the warlike', 'the conquering'. There was nothing to do but defiantly adopt the planet's name. Cairo, Al-Qahira, has ridden the omens.

The dynasty of Al-Mo'izz had many unusual characteristics. For one thing, the Fatimids were Arabs, not Turks. For another they delighted in art as well as in science. The fact that they were Shiites cut the Fatimids off from the rest of orthodox Islam. Their arts show a free, sensuous line unknown in other Arab epochs and equalled only in Shiite Persia. Instead of arid arabesque, Fatimid ceramics carry portraits of lute-players with bunches of grapes, huge eyes and turbans: also animals. A fine collection of these ceramics is in the Islamic Museum.

Speed and energy were also Fatimid characteristics. We come to an example as we walk north, through the middle of the quadrilateral. The very year after the foundation of the city, on 3rd April, Gawhar laid the foundations of Al-Azhar, the university mosque at the eastern side of the Fatimid capital. Two years later the building was finished. Students were admitted in 968.

To this day the Fatimid city—blurred though it is at most of its edges, confused inside by later additions that range from courtly Mameluke houses with inner gardens to hideous apartment blocks—is the part of Cairo which has most magic. Critics often complain that the Egyptians have not preserved enough of the old. Sixty years ago, according to Stanley Lane Poole, 'the department which attends to the alignment of the streets has often exercised its powers in the narrowest spirit of county-councildom'. But no living city—particularly no capital—can afford to keep its heart an embalmed Williamsburg. Children need education; how can schools be built fast without concrete and iron bars? There are enough fragments left for those with imagination to recreate much of the past. And the road to follow now is the road which leads from Bab Zuweyla in the south to Bab al-Nasr in the north. The best companion to take is Mrs Devonshire's *Rambles in Cairo*. Least pretentious of dragomans and best informed, Mrs Devonshire guides one surely, in flat, reliable prose, to the secret hiding-places of the past. For those who have a week or more to spend in old Cairo she can uncover the treasures which this chapter must ignore. But to return, leaving the great hospital of Qalawun and the other splendid monuments of Mameluke times, and to tread today the road 'between the two palaces' which links Bab Zuweyla and Bab al-Nasr: at the end of the crowded, exhausting, rewarding walk, under the very shadow of great walls, is a third great mosque, that of Al-Hakim.

Here some criticism might be given to the guardians of the

Islamic past. The great mosque of Al-Hakim (his full name meant 'He who rules in the order of God') was originally called the 'New Mosque', or the 'Brilliant'. Immeasureably tired, dusty, it stands just inside the northern entrance to the Fatimid city. (The walls are the mosque's defence. The best place to see the mosque is from the towers that mark the Bab al-Nasr, or 'Gate of Triumph'.) If an admirer of the Arabs were asked what the Arabs have achieved, this ruin would be his first choice to point at—at least in Cairo. The city has other, grander mosques. The unique distinction of Al-Hakim is that it was built for an Arab. Yet the mosque is neglected. After centuries of ill-usage it had a major fire early this century. Repairs have been scanty. Much of the Kufic plastering has fallen. Yet two minarets emerge from receding square towers, slender, vast and intricate. Below them the forest of brick aisles has decayed; a school of no distinction fills one corner.

I suggested to an Arab nationalist that, in a city acclaimed as the heart of Arabism, this mosque should be tended, not neglected. He replied: 'Perhaps it is neglected because of the hatred people still feel for Al-Hakim.'

Al-Hakim, besides being the grandson of Al-Mo'izz, was also the Arab Caligula: spoilt, egotistical, rational and insane by turns, tolerant and intolerant, he caused misery in *trivia*, in *gravia*, before he died, anonymously murdered when out on a desert donkey ride. His victims were the Copts, whom he massacred, the sellers of *malukhiya* (a slimy vegetable dish still loved by Cairenes), whose cooking he forbade, brewers, shoemakers (he banned women's shoes to enforce a day-and-night curfew) and players of chess. One final category of victim will kill Anglo-Saxon sympathy: he ordered the slaughter of the dogs of Cairo. There must have been some grandeur in this self-deifying monster, for the Druses of Lebanon still revere him as an avatar of virtue. Yet his eerie mosque is a place I should hesitate to enter at night. Even by day bats as big as pheasants swoop in the square tower through which

Harim windows in the seventeenth-century Mameluke
house of Gamal al-Din al-Dhahaby (*page 13*). Note the delicate
meshrebiya grille-work, through which the women could
look out without being seen

△ Nubian *farah,* a wedding party

◁ Dancer at Rukn al Rif, a nig club specializi in village entertain- ments

Weaving car-
pets in street-side
shoplets (*page 47*)

Coptic wed-
ding: the Copts
have never married
with Arabs or
Turks, and so pre-
serve the blood of
the Pharaonic
Egyptians

Inside a small
mosque near the
Virgin's Tree,
Mattaria, sacred
to Mary's sojourn
in Egypt

◁ Florid
Turkish *sebeel*
(*page 47*), an
Ottoman fantasy

Tombs beneath the Mokattam hills (*page 25*), where clings the ruined mosque of Shahin al-Khalwati (1538) ▷

' Popular housing ' in a former slum area near the aqueduct ▽

△ Al-Tahrir bridge, looking east
▽ Abdin Square at dawn: religious oration,
speaker attacking superstition

A street in
Old Cairo
▷

Al-Azhar, millennial Islamic university, educational magnet for Muslim Africa (*pages 66 to 68*)

the minaret rises to its decorative summit. The noise of the bats
obliterates the noise of the traffic.

Al-Hakim's mosque is the last of a series and a kind. Like
Amr's, like Ibn Tulun's, it seems to exhibit a religious faith on the
attack, a faith that was in one sense democratic: for in the mosque
there were no favourites, though the sultan or caliph rode up
to the mosque gorgeously caparisoned and resolutely guarded.
(Killings in mosques have been an odious tradition, from that of
Ali praying in Kufa to King Abdullah arriving to pray in Jeru-
salem.) But these great mosques were also military, male. The
devout were still the people in arms. 'The people' meant 'the
Muslims': there was at this time no more Arab or Turkish
nationalism than there was French or German nationalism in
Christian Europe. Behind the Leader of the Faithful the serried
masses would pray, prostrating themselves to God, repeating the
phrases of the Arabian Prophet.

Already in Al-Hakim's mosque there is a hint of change. We
know that the caliph was insane; a despot. We know that already
the bodyguard (for whom whole quarters of the city had been
designed) were becoming as powerful as the man they guarded.
Already the diminution of the caliph, his reduction to a nonentity,
seems to be hinted by a certain delicacy in the arches. Already
there is something graceful to the point of femininity, a certain
withdrawal from the robust spirit which finds, more than anywhere else on earth, its manifestation in the great plastered piers
of Ibn Tulun. There are already hints in Al-Hakim of an Islam on
the defensive, of a turning inwards. (The Fatimid dynasty expired
when the Crusaders briefly occupied Cairo in 1163.) The caliphate
no longer meant what it had done in the early centuries when the
Muslims rode east and west, confident that the limits of their
realm would be the limits of the world. Defeated at the extremities
of their empire, they were divided within. The Fatimid caliph was
only one among several claimants. His claims were not recognized
in Baghdad or Andaluz.

E

So we must take a taxi abruptly from Al-Hakim's mosque. We can tell it to pause a moment, its meter ticking, at Al-Aqmar, the best preserved of the Fatimid mosques in Cairo, a few hundred yards from Al-Hakim, back along the road between the two palaces we have already trod. A severe façade has the Fatimid lightness of decoration. But we do not linger. The day advances and we tell the driver (who will be pleased with a tip of one or two piastres) to go to Sultan Hassan.

The tomb-mosque of Sultan Hassan shows that Islam has changed—as a culture, if not as a doctrine—and that its buildings have changed, too, in form and spirit. This mosque is as religious as that of Ibn Tulun. Indeed its tunnelled entrance has something of the Pharaonic gloom that was designed to induce awe and hair-standing horror in the worshipper. And, like the Pharaonic faith, Sultan Hassan's mosque is a giant preparation for a small man's death. Past the tunnel, whose entrance is a resonant porchway hung with carved stalactites, a vast courtyard is open to the sky; but the sky is far above; for this *sahn* is surrounded, not by a forest of shadow, but by four great naves, arched and sombre. Beyond the east nave, beyond the niche that shows the direction of Mecca, is not void and Arabia, but a vast tomb-chamber. The tomb itself is empty. It was designed for a fourteenth-century ruler, Sultan Hassan, as insignificant as Tutankhamen or Iraq's King Feisal II. He was the seventh of the eight sons of Al-Nasir Muhammad, a Mameluke of more than usual authority. But Hassan, despite a liking for native Egyptian Muslims and a prejudice against Copts, achieved no popular basis from which to control his country. Nevertheless he has given his name to what is an architectural masterpiece—and a clue at the same time to the state of Islam in the later Middle Ages. The mosque is not only death-centred, though the provision of a splendid tomb was its main purpose. At the side of each of the four gigantic arches that lead into the *sahn* are the doorways to four schoolrooms, each set aside for the use of one of the four schools of Sunnite Islam, whose

differences are infinitesimal compared with the difference, for
example, between Baptist and Methodist, or for that matter
between Sunnite and Shiite Muslim. Yet though education was
fostered in the schools, and hygiene at the central fountain, there
is a turning inwards that is symbolical. For all his affection for the
Egyptians, Sultan Hassan was a Mameluke, an alien. The Mamelukes, whether vigorous and constructive or weak and capricious,
were never one with their people. In the mosque of Sultan Hassan
we have travelled far from the spirit of Amr, improvising a city of
tents, running up a simple mosque for his soldiers, *primus inter
pares*. Amr had come from the Arabia of Muhammad, where the
Prophet darned his own clothes in a simple house, where women
took part in battles and literary circles. Sultan Hassan was in a
tradition which had developed the enclosed *harim*. In his mosque
we are in the world of royalty, almost of Windsor.

The last stage in our day's journey takes us into the cemeteries
east of the city. Here are the preoccupations of the later Mamelukes, their tombs. Without schools or fountains these places are
entirely for death. Many are beautiful, many crumbling. Domes
and more domes are the features of the necropolis. Nearby, the
vast rubbish dumps are being planted with trees, but round the
tombs themselves there is persistent dust. Which tomb shall we
enter? If it is open, that of Qayt Bey, one of the most energetic
Mamelukes of the period immediately preceding the Turkish
conquest. A feature of his domed mausoleum is the stained glass
high up in the walls which lets in a light that is not of Egypt.

So much dust, so much death: your nostrils are clogged, your
spirits begin to feel that everything is beige. To conclude the day's
journey you will perhaps take a *felucca* on the Nile, to let the cool
north wind rout depression and quicken an appetite for evening.
In the *felucca* you will see, as the sun sinks, a new mosque where a
bridge joins Roda to Giza. It is named after Saladin. Floodlit to
icing sugar, it shows that Cairo has its Pugins, its equivalent of the
Anglican revival of perpendicular Gothic.

Chapter 12

Nocturnal

CAIRO nights are more memorable than Cairo days; they are incomparably more dramatic than nights in Europe. Part is climate. In winter (when day temperatures may be around sixty) and in summer (when they may soar above a hundred) there is a dramatic drop in temperatures as soon as the sun subsides behind the Pyramids. Because the air is so dry the stars seem more numerous and more lustrous than in damper climes. As the city's two thousand night guards—elderly men with elderly rifles—patrol the transmuted streets, what pleasures of the night does Cairo offer?

Cairo has sixteen restaurants by the Nile. Some are on houseboats, some in gardens. As it rains for only a few minutes every year, these open-air restaurants stay open all the year round— though in winter the nights can be chill. My own favourite riverside restaurant is the Casino des Pigeons on the west bank, in Giza. Giza is a separate governorate from Cairo, with a separate governor. In the holy month of Ramadan, when pious Muslims neither eat nor drink in daylight hours, the governor of Giza forbids the sale of alcohol. (Cairo's governor allows it.) For the other months of the year you can drink beer, *zebeeb*,[1] or Egyptian wine. 'The juice of Egypt's grape' deserves to be better known than it is. The Gianiclis estate in the Delta produces a wide range of red and white wines which are moderate in price and certainly better than much of the *vin ordinaire* in France. The best red is called

[1] *Zebeeb* is the Egyptian version of the colourless drink which turns white when mixed with water. Known as *ouzo* in Greece, *raki* in Turkey, its name in other Arab countries is *araq*.

56

Omar Khayyam, the best white, Clos Nestor. The only thing to eat with the wine—the pigeons (in Arabic *hamam*) which give the restaurant its name. They are grilled on charcoal, and while you eat them a regiment of cats, scrawny descendants of those worshipped by the Pharaohs, patiently watch you. Overhead tall eucalyptuses rustle; beside you, almost within touching distance, *feluccas* and sail-drawn barges of freight pass to and fro.

Cairo is not a city for fussy gastronomes. Its restaurants, particularly those in the modern hotels, serve standard Western food which ranges from good to mediocre. Plates are usually cold, even for omelettes; if you persist, as I do, in asking for hot plates, you are likely to be served with plates too hot to touch and then be kept waiting for the food. The ban on importing luxuries means that such things as French or Italian cheeses are unavailable. But Egyptian meat is good, particularly lamb, and the fish from the Mediterranean and the Red Sea can be excellent. The high proportion of phosphorus in the Red Sea is said to be the reason why the Suez prawns are so gigantic.

Eastern modes of cooking can be sampled in *baladi* restaurants. If Paris is the focus of European cooking, Istanbul is the focus for the food cooked, not only in Turkey itself, but in all the former provinces of the Ottoman Empire—Greece, Syria, Lebanon and Egypt. I should place Egyptian food higher than Greek and a little lower than Lebanese. In the *baladi* restaurants the best meat dishes are *kufta* and *kebab*. Both derive from lamb: in the case of *kufta* the lamb is minced and grilled on a skewer; in the case of *kebab*, little portions of meat are grilled separately. Also worth trying are *malukhia*, the slimy vegetable banned by the mad Caliph Al-Hakim, and, from a little restaurant near Bab al-Louk, fried brains and liver. *Kawarma*—a dish made from the feet of quadrupeds—has never passed my lips; I therefore cannot recommend it.

For those who want to eat economically—and this is something most Cairenes have to do most of the time—many clean little

restaurants sell *ful mudammas* (page 48) and *tac'amia*. *Tac'amia* are
little balls of breadcrumbs, *fava* beans, herbs and onions, enlivened
with yeast, sprinkled with sesame seeds and fried in oil. In these
places one can have a filling meal, including the round *baladi* bread
and a salad, for less than a shilling.

Having eaten—and it is the Cairo custom to make up in quantity for any lack in quality—what does one do next?

To the ordinary Cairene several answers are possible. If one is
a woman, one usually sits at home, sewing, watching television or
simply talking to other women. If one is a man, one goes to one's
favourite among the city's six thousand cafés. In the cafés the
drink is tea, the amusement either *tawla* (the Egyptian back-
gammon), television or talking. The Cairo pleasures are largely
sessile, though young people belong to sporting clubs or throng
the pavements outside the cinemas.

Thursday night is 'cinema night' *par excellence*, for Friday is the
Muslim day of rest. Cairo has ninety-two cinemas from which to
choose. Dostoyevsky, describing a play put on in a Czarist prison
in Siberia, long ago noted: 'All Mohammedans love a spectacle.'
This was a true observation. No cities have more persistent film
fans than the Arab capitals, and Cairo is the one Arab city with a
major film industry. The Cairo studios—situated by a canal near
the Pyramids—have produced films since the twenties.[1] In some
years the production has been greater than that of Britain. *Avant-
garde* directors like Yusif Shaheen deplore a quantity which leaves
quality impoverished or shivering. The cinema has been Egypt's
'formula art'—as rigid as the *Commedia dell'Arte*. My own
experience of the industry was when its capitalist nature was still
strident. A woman friend passed me an invitation to lunch from
one of Cairo's senior producers. A Shami, he had started life
designing hair-styles for Levantine women ('Justine' may have
been one of his clients) but now devoted himself to designing
dreams for the Arab millions.

[1] The earliest feature, *Mr So-and-So at the Seaside* (1919).

'I need a story, Mr Stewart, for our two big stars, Faten
Hamama and Shadia. As they take half the budget between them,
it must be something new.' I had already seen the two ladies
concerned. Faten, married to Omar Sherif, who played the Arab
sheikh in *Lawrence of Arabia*, is probably Egypt's sincerest
actress; Shadia seemed a frivolous, pretty creature with a thin
voice.

'Something realistic?'

'Mr Stewart!' Manicured hands flew upwards in horror.
'*Please!* Our people are poor and they need to dream. We have
had enough of realism.'

This was hardly true, from what I had seen of Egyptian films;
but that month I was poor, as my woman friend knew, and the
sum offered seemed adequate for twenty pages. A friend warned
me: 'Be careful, they will pay at every stage except the last.' This
proved correct. I got the first instalments in unwilling driblets;
the producer was either 'sleeping' or 'in Syria' when I tele-
phoned; but when my story was complete and a third of the
money remained to be paid, I was told in hurt tones: 'But my son
could have jotted on two sheets of paper what you have written
on twenty; and your English—my daughter is student at the
American university, she say: "Mr Stewart write good English,
but not English English."'

What could I do? I was not proud of my unrealistic script. Had
I not, in one scene, shown Shadia, childless, weeping, a baby-book
open beside her on a Louise Seize settee?

In fact, when the formula has been brushed aside—tears
therein are dissolved in smiles, young officers with cars or private
aeroplanes wind up plots embellished by song and dance—both
Faten and Shadia have acted well. Faten played in *The Call of the
Curlew*, an Upper Egyptian tragedy by the blind author Taha
Hussein. Her sister had been betrayed by a lawyer and she set out
to avenge her. For the first hour the setting was realistic, down to
bare feet and anklets for the women—something unheard of

before. The last hour saw a collapse, with the lawyer and Faten (now dressed like a young lady from Zamalek) picnicking together by a lake: something unimaginable in conservative Upper Egypt. More recently Shadia was cast as the prostitute in what, to my mind, is the best Egyptian film yet made, *The Thief and the Dogs*. This story was written by Naguib Mahfouz round a press-hunted villain, the Slayer, a deranged assassin who specialized in disguises and who was finally shot down like Dillinger. To Mahfouz, the Slayer becomes the symbol of modern man betrayed by his guides. By a miracle, the film intruded no cosy comfort, no kindly police officer suggesting that 'we now set to and build Arab socialism'. The scenario was quick-moving, not particularly talkative; ruthless, exciting. The motivation was without platitude. The hero has been put on the road to crime by a cynical leftist in whose student-hostel he worked as a servant. The student has purveyed the notions, stale in the West but still novel in Egypt, that morality is old-hat and that in a capitalist society the thief is a progressive figure. The leftist turns into a successful journalist and leads the hue and cry against his innocent-hearted disciple. The journalist smiles when, mourned only by the whore, the killer is shot down by police machine-guns at the foot of the Giyushi Mosque.

There are signs that the old 'formula' is losing its hold. Arguments have appeared in the press against its main prop, the star system in which, as my producer friend had told me, two actresses can consume half the meagre budget (around £25,000) of a picture, leaving little for scenarists and other artists of talent. The stars are seldom of much value, being self-lighted and without the training which a repertory theatre could provide. Young actors whose looks appeal to the public can jump from a fee of £150 for a first picture to £2,000 for a second. Unless, like Omar Sherif, they have real talent, flattery often turns their head for life.

The salvation of the Cairo cinema—and perhaps its eventual break-through to quality worthy of international appreciation—

may come through the theatrical renaissance which is, perhaps, the major cultural phenomenon in the Cairo of the early sixties. Although there has been a theatre of sorts in Egypt since the end of the nineteenth century, in 1952 there were only two serious theatres in Cairo. There are now no less than eighteen theatrical troupes with fourteen theatre buildings. This number promises to increase even further. The plays which are put on range from domestic comedies with titles such as *Papa Doesn't Know* to translations of Beckett and Ionesco. In addition to the Pocket Theatre, which specializes in the international *avant-garde*, the new 'Towfik al-Hakim Theatre' has been created to stage the dramas of Egypt's foremost dramatist. An academy of dramatic art is turning out young actors, all of whom have been guaranteed jobs by the energetic Deputy Prime Minister, Dr Abdel Kader Hatem. The minister's approach to culture was defined to me in an interview for the B.B.C. high up in the television building by the Nile.

'Since the Revolution,' Dr Hatem said, 'a purely Egyptian government has ruled the country for the first time since the Middle Ages. The aim of the government is to spread a cultural minimum amongst all our people. The fact that a man lives in Aswan, or even Siwa Oasis, is no reason why he should not learn about the modern world—by reading a newspaper or even watching television. We are not ashamed that our stress is on quantity, because we believe that when all our people can read and write and participate in a minimum level of culture, then we shall have the basis of a pyramid whose apex will be of the highest quality.'

This conscious attempt to make Cairo the point of diffusion of a nation-wide culture is shown in music: above all, in song. The Arabs have always been masters—and victims—of the word. Poetry was the great art of the desert; in sophisticated Egypt the songs of Ahmed Showky and Ahmed Ramy have reached mass audiences through the voice of one woman, Um Kalthum. Now in her early sixties, Um Kalthum has admirers all over the Arab world. She sings on the first Thursday of every month, and from Baghdad to Morocco crowded cafés wait for the new song. In Cairo, not far from Midan Towfikiah, is the 'Um Kalthum Café'. This café has three floors. The ground floor, open to the street, is a normal Cairo café, brightly lit, noisy. The first floor is dark. Here is set the tape-recorder from which swirls out the oceanic voice of Um Kalthum. Here young men—students, government officials, soldiers—sit quietly with a cup of coffee by the hour. On the top floor the atmosphere is darker. Here, mouse-quiet, are the addicts. Here even to whisper would be a sacrilege.

Dr Hatem's encouragement of the popular arts also includes an element not so much of censorship as of tidying up. The Ministry of Culture represents, in Freudian terms, the Superego controlling the Id. The Id is the vast irrepressible unconscious of the people. This tidying up has applied to dancing. In Lane's time (the early nineteenth century) there were dancers of two kinds. First, the Ghawazees. These were women of a special tribe who danced in the costume of the fashionable Turkish ladies of the day: voluminous pantaloons, a waistcoat and sash, and over these, a long *kaftan* with slashed dependent sleeves. On their heads they wore flat caps. These dancers, whose origins Lane traced back to Roman times, were in demand at weddings to perform before the male guests. 'Their dancing has little elegance,' wrote the prudish Lane; 'its chief peculiarity being a very rapid vibrating motion of the hips from side to side.'

Because there has always been a puritan streak in Islam—which objected to woman performing before men, even when they came from a tribe immemorially dedicated to this profession—the second tribe of dancers were considered more decent by certain moralists. These were the Khawals, male dancers who dressed as women. 'They are Muslims, and natives of Egypt. As they personate women, their dances are exactly of the same description as those of the Ghawazee; and are, in like manner, accompanied by the sound of castanets; but, as if to prevent their being thought

to be really females, their dress is suited to their unnatural profession, being partly male and partly female; it chiefly consists of
a tight vest, a girdle, and a kind of petticoat. Their general
appearance, however, is more feminine than masculine: they
suffer the hair of the head to grow long, and generally braid it, in
the manner of the women; the hair on the face, when it begins to
grow, they pluck out; and they imitate the women also in applying
kohl and henna to their eyes and hands. In the streets, when not
engaged in dancing, they often veil their faces; not from shame,
but merely to affect the manners of women. They are often
employed, in preference to the Ghawazee, to dance before a house,
or in its court, on the occasion of a marriage-fête, or the birth of
a child, or a circumcision; and frequently perform at public
festivals.'

The Eastern belly-dance of modern night-clubs (Cairo has
twenty-five) is the *fin-de-siècle* development of Ghawazee dancing.
The costume, far from being traditional, is a travesty of what
European costume-designers thought to be Eastern, and possibly
dates from the ballerina's appearance in *Aida*. The costume allows
display of a bare midriff between brass pectorals and a diaphanous
skirt. In the days of Farouk, very tiny gold coins would be
thrown on to the floor by the girl's admirers; these would then be
sewn into the skirt like sequins; they were as thin as tinfoil.

The bare midriff was one of the first victims of the Superego. A
post-revolutionary edict decreed that henceforth the stomach was
to be covered with net or gauze. An attempt (quite vain) has been
made by some theoreticians to evolve a 'pure' art form from this
sensual dance, which even at its worst takes a thrilling *tempo* from
the blood-rhythms of a flagellated drum. Musicians are often
blind. The belly-dance can still be seen, not in the Hilton night-
club, but at any local wedding where bare abdomen swirls and
where gestures are still what they always were. Male dancers in
female clothes can still be hired. They often wear a moustache as
well as plucked eyebrows and long tresses. The modern name for

these transvestites is 'Abu'lgheit', for the term 'Khawal' is now
an insult.

If the Ghawazees and the transvestites are manifestations of the
Id, the Reda Troupe of folklore dancers are approved by the
Superego. Just after Egypt recognized communist China, the
Peking Opera visited Cairo. The Chinese ambassador on that
occasion invited a 'troupe of Egyptian dancers' to visit his
country. This invitation caused momentary embarrassment. To
export a group of Ghawazees and Khawals was unthinkable; but
no other troupe existed. With praiseworthy haste a troupe was
created by Mahmoud Reda and his sister-in-law Ferida Fahmy.
Their troupe is popular in the sense of being liked. Originally a
band of university students (Mahmoud had danced for a year in
Paris with the Argentine ballet of Alfredo Alaria), the group is now
referred to as the 'U.A.R. folk ballet'. According to the *Arab
Observer*: 'Last year the company presented its first full-size
ballet, *The Bride of the Nile*, the story of a village Romeo and
Juliet, but with a happy ending. This became the *pièce de résistance*
of the company's tour through Germany, Yugoslavia and the
U.S.S.R., with performances in twenty-seven cities. In Yugoslavia, the company participated in a folk-dance festival and was
awarded first prize.'

A similar metamorphosis has overtaken Karagoz, the 'Punch
and Judy' of the East. Karagoz, or 'Black Eyes' in Turkish, was
the architect of Saladin; but the origins of the popular art named
after him are lost in the steppes towards China. In Lane's time
Karagoz shows were 'conducted in the manner of the "Chinese
shadows" and therefore only exhibited at night.' A beautiful set of
Karagoz figures was unearthed in the oasis of Fayum (an hour's
drive south of Cairo) and is now in Berlin. They had been made in
the sixteenth century for the entertainment of a Mameluke Bey.
To see Karagoz in his original form as a shadow-play one now has
to go to Peiraeus in Greece. Transparent tinted figures made of
parchment enact comedies which are often bawdy. In Cairo the

name Karagoz survives for a noisy 'Punch and Judy' show which tours the streets along with tumblers and the winders of hurdy-gurdies, the latter embellished with tinted photographs of Neapolitan beauties. Two such practitioners of this glove-puppet art are known to me. Their high-pitched screaming quickly draws a crowd to their gaudy booths. So real is the impudent puppet that a child will dash forward to pinch him below the navel, to the sedate amusement of coffee-slurpers on café terraces.

But just as the Ghawazees and Khawals have been tidied into the folk-ballet, so Karagoz has been developed into a puppet theatre under the patronage of the Ministry of Culture. Controlled lighting and the solemnity of a small theatre give some advantages. In January 1963 Cairo's best and fattest cartoonist, Salah Jaheen, was the author of *The Donkey of Shehab al-Din*, a fairy tale set in a Baghdad recreated in the best Wardour Street tradition. The lighting was pretty; the puppets well managed. But despite Jaheen's excellence, not only as a cartoonist but as vernacular poet, the auspices under which the play was produced ruled out obscenity, violence and wit. A lethal air of reverence killed the vigour which remains the asset of the street-performer. For the latter, benefiting from no governmental subsidy, remembers, or knows instinctively, the axiom of Durranty, the great nineteenth-century puppet-master: what puppets do is more important than what they say.

Chapter 13

Didactic

CAIRO has been for a thousand years the chief educational centre in Africa. Admittedly this superlative at times meant little, since the places of African education were few. For the last hundred years it has meant a great deal.

Cairo's educational supremacy derives from the foundation of Al-Azhar the year after the Fatimid occupation of Egypt. So vital has this mosque-university been to Egypt, Islam and Africa that here, perhaps, is the place to write its founder's name in full: Jawhar al-Katib al-Sikilli. The Egyptians, who pronounce the *jeem* of classical Arabic as *geem*, know him as Gawhar.

Gawar's Al-Azhar has enormously expanded throughout succeeding centuries. His mosque had a curious talisman on the tops of three columns: bird-figures intended to prevent real birds from nesting inside the building. Just as the Oxford colleges were originally built round churches and chapels (with living quarters for the students coming as an afterthought later) so the mosque was always the hub of Al-Azhar. The noise of birds would disturb the lecturers. But while Oxford, born later than Al-Azhar, developed rapidly after the sixteenth century, for nine centuries Al-Azhar seemed to stagnate; tradition overlay vitality. Much of the tradition was good. (Even today the visitor can see a professor surrounded by a respectful knot of students on the carpets of the great mosque.) But the curriculum they studied was narrow and scholastic—the different ways of reciting the Koran, the *hadith*, or Sayings of the Prophet, Arabic grammar and Muslim jurisprudence.

The students themselves were divided into territorial groups. Each group would have its student-room and loggia, or apportioned space between the pillars.[1] Up till the nineteenth century the main groups remained as follows: the Saidis, or Upper Egyptians; the Meccans and Medinans; the Sudanese from Darfur; the Syrians; the Javanese; the Afghanis; the North Africans; the Somalis; the Turks; the Kurds; the Indians; the Baghdadis; the Nubians; and those from the Oasis of Fayum. The Iranians did not come, for they remained Shiite, while, after the overthrow of the Fatimids, Al-Azhar, a Shiite foundation, had reverted to Sunnite orthodoxy. Hardly any institution in the world can have had—or can have—as catholic a student body. The effect of Al-Azhar—even when it was stagnant—was immense, for the religious leaders of Muslim communities everywhere looked to Al-Azhar as the fountain of orthodoxy.

There have been two main stages in the modernization of Al-Azhar. The first was undertaken by Muhammad Abdu in the last decade of the nineteenth century. He put the professors on to regular stipends, and as a result of his efforts faculties were introduced. The second attempt has been made since the revolution of 1952. President Nasser's government realized that the graduates of Al-Azhar were going back to every corner of Africa and Asia equipped merely to teach religion and Arabic grammar. It was felt by Nasser and his advisers that Azhar graduates should be able to take the lead in their communities, not merely by teaching theology, but by teaching those practical techniques and disciplines which developing societies require. For the good of Islam as a whole, Al-Azhar needed to become a progressive instead of a reactionary institution. As a result there has been something parallel to the 'worker priest' movement in Catholicism. Engineering and sciences are now taught to Azhar students. Girls have been admitted—something unimaginable even a generation ago. In 1964 a radical new step was announced: a project for a new

[1] The student-room was called *hāra*; the loggia *riwāq*.

Azhar on a 500-acre site in Nasr City, a rapidly growing administrative suburb north of Abbasia. At Kubba another 150 acres will be given for an Islamic girls' college linked with Al-Azhar.

This transformation of Al-Azhar with its more than 40,000 primary, secondary and undergraduate students has been due in part to the challenge of a parallel, totally lay system of education. While one stream of Cairo students continued to wear *kaftans* and turbans and to study a scholastic curriculum hardly changed from the Middle Ages, another, in Western clothes, studied nuclear science and political economy. There was little or no interfusion between the two streams.

The schism between these two approaches to education goes back to the military schools of Muhammad Ali. The schism widened throughout the nineteenth century, from the foundation of the Dar al-'Ilum (or 'House of Sciences') in 1873 to the establishment of the Fuad I University in 1927. Feeding these higher institutions was a system of primary and secondary education which is now compulsory and free. A higher proportion of schoolchildren go on to universities than in contemporary Britain, though this is not to imply that the standard in the universities is as high—it is not. But statistics for 1963–4 are revealing. There were 608,000 children in school in Cairo; of these 262,000 were girls. In two of Cairo four universities ('Cairo', no longer called after Fuad I, and 'Ain Shems') there were a total of 72,913 undergraduate students; of these just over 16,000 were women. While these figures show that women are still under-represented in the Cairo educational system, they also show a truly remarkable quantitative expansion. The women who are playing an increasingly active role in Egyptian life (the best known is Hikmat Abu Zaid, the Minister of Social Affairs) are all graduates of these universities. One of Hikmat Abu Zaid's current tasks is that of organizing 700 birth-control centres throughout the republic.

That Cairo sees itself as the educational centre of Africa is shown, not merely by the provision of tens of thousands of scholarships to African young men and women, but by the didactic (I use the word advisedly) use of the Egyptian radio. 'The Voice of Africa from Cairo' broadcasts daily in Amharic, Swahili, Lingala, Sesotho, Nyanja, Somali, Fulani, Hausa and, for those who do not speak these languages, in English and French.

Chapter 14

Pharaonic

THIS can be a short negative chapter. Cairo is not a Pharaonic city. Of course, just as London houses the Elgin Marbles, Cairo's Museum—in Liberation Square, north-east of the Hilton—houses the most splendid collection of Pharaonic antiquities in the world. For two piastres [1] you can visit more than a hundred rooms containing the relics of a civilization as old as urban man. A never-ending stream of visitors from all over the planet file past the grave-furniture of Tutankhamen or confront the mummies of Ramses II and Seti I. (Under Farouk the mummies were secluded from the gaze of tourists; the king considered the Pharaohs as his predecessors, and gaping as *lèse-majesté*. The democratic republic charges an extra five shillings to enter Room 52, where the mummies are on view.) Cairenes are proud of their Museum; they realize that it is a major reason why 400,000 people visit their city annually. But the names over the Museum are not those of Egyptians. The museum was founded in 1857 by Auguste Mariette, a Frenchman; the present building was planned by Marcel Bourgnon. Egyptology, the study started by such Europeans as Champollion and Mariette, has only recently engrossed Egyptians.

If Cairo itself is an Islamic and not a Pharaonic city, it is a splendid centre for Pharaonic studies. Even for the casual tourist a major attraction is its proximity to Giza and Sakkara. At the

[1] The Egyptian pound, or guinea, is divided into a thousand milliemes, or a hundred piastres. While the £1E goes further in Cairo than £1 in London, its value on the international black market is considerably lower. Within Egypt £1 is exchanged for £1E and five shillings.

Pyramids a nightly performance of *Son et Lumière* evokes the
millennia before the Ptolemies. The Sphinx, cleared of sand,
receives the morning sun on his royal brow as he stares detachedly
towards the city. From the new suburbs on the Mokattam hills
you can see families of pyramids as far as the eye can stretch to the
south. If you arrive at Cairo station from Alexandria or Port Said,
you see, outside, a mammoth statue of Ramses II. Discovered
near Sakkara, the Pharaoh stands lonely and upright, jets of water
cascading from his feet.

But in Cairo the main influence of the Pharaohs is an imitation
of their motifs in certain restaurants and on certain textiles.

But I am wrong. One positive element *is* Pharaonic—the young
women who with kohl enlarge their already enormous eyes and
with some mysterious art contrive to make their dark hair hang
like the wig which Nofret,[1] sitting beside her husband Prince
Rahotep, wears eternally.

---

[1] Cairo Museum; ground floor, Room 32.

Chapter 15

Political

THE political aspect of Cairo—capital of Egypt, 'heart of Arabism', secretariat of Afro-Asia—is not least important. For one thing, the political aspect conditions so much else. The tourist industry—its revenues marching with those of the Suez Canal—flourishes as relations improve with the outside world. On the other hand, a political crisis can empty a hotel. The cotton crop—still the country's main earner of foreign currency—goes west, or east, as politics dictate.

Cairo is the capital of a traditionally centralized country. To offset this a republican decree has given far greater scope to provincial governors; the industrial development of Cairo's outer satellite Helwan, as well as the development of Aswan, has been an attempt to give Egypt other focuses of power. Yet nowhere in the world is the capital more magnetic. The very word '*Masr*' means both Cairo *and* Egypt. To a Cairene, Mersa Matruh (except in August) still spells exile.

Cairo's role as source of power was shown in its Citadel, then in the various palaces used by Egypt's kings. Yet Cairo has for a century and a half possessed some form of parliament. Napoleon initiated an assembly of notables; under Ismail a limited parliament was established; between the two world wars the parliament was loquacious but ineffective. As in other Middle Eastern countries the landlords controlled the elections and the deputies never tackled such basic problems as land reform.

The socialist laws that have followed the revolution of 1952 have been the result of decrees, not debates. At the same time there have been three attempts to fill the parliament building with worthy representatives. The first was the Liberation Rally; it failed. The second was the National Union; it collapsed with the collapse of the union between Egypt and Syria. The 360 members of the new National Assembly met for the first time in the spring of 1964. This new 'parliament'—all of whose members belong to the Arab Socialist Union—is the result of the profound heart-searching (and head-searching) which followed the Syrian secession in 1961. Nasser and his people probed for the reasons why there had been no popular resistance to the secession, no organizations capable of maintaining a union which most Arabs wanted, and perhaps still want. The new assembly has certain interesting features. One stipulation of the 'National Charter'—a long basic document approved by a Congress of Popular Powers in 1963—is that at least 50 per cent of all members of the National Assembly must be workers and *fellahin*. Critics have argued that it is as easy to hand-pick people in *gallabya* and overalls as people in lounge suits. But such criticism overlooks an important fact. The workers and *fellahin* are more independent in spirit than those who slurp coffee in Cairo offices. If even a minority of the National Assembly express their opinions and criticisms as frankly as they do in their cafés, Egypt will have a parliament of utmost interest to those concerned with human freedom in Afro-Asia. For in many newly independent countries there has been a rejection, overt or covert, of the Western system of parliamentary democracy. The assertion that the British or French system may not suit those with different traditions and urgent problems may be valid; it rings more convincingly, however, when made by those sincerely attempting to produce a substitute.

If the National Assembly is the great hope for a democratic Egypt, Cairo is also the lair of a formidable challenge: the bureaucracy. A huge building in Stalin-Allee concrete, the Mugamaa, symbolizes this challenge, for it is here that citizens must go for countless forms and permits. Under the monarchy the bureaucracy was notoriously venal and lazy. But the bureaucracy did not then concern most of the people very intimately. Under Nasser's Arab Socialism the bureaucracy is larger and more influential. As the state controls more of the citizen's life—for his own benefit in most cases—the importance of having polite, efficient public servants becomes greater. In the past the bureaucrats made up for their low wages by taking bribes and tyrannizing the public. Can public service become a sufficient motive to the bureaucrats, and can the old schism between 'them' and 'us' be abolished? I leave this rhetorical question not for the orators but for the historians of the immediate future.

If the bureaucrats are dangerous from an excess of petty power, another kind of public servant for long seemed impotent. Cairo has been, since 1947, the headquarters of the Arab League. No sooner was the League born than it was faced with a problem which it could not solve. The Palestine defeat in 1948 discredited not only the Arab governments, which had failed to support the Arab majority in Palestine effectively, but also the League. Consequent bickerings between different Arab regimes was followed by a clash between revolutionary governments (as these took power in one Arab country after another) and old-fashioned despotisms. For many years the Arab League building by the Nile seemed an ideological white elephant, its Andalusian architecture pathetically nostalgic for an age when Arabs could act, not only talk.

As ineffective as his organization seemed Abdel Khalek Hassouna, the apparently perpetual secretary-general of the League. Hassouna is in every sense a man of the old school. He still dislikes being referred to by any title other than Hassouna Pasha. In an age of verbal violence he spoke in moderate platitudes; his manners were excellent. Behind the platitudes was a belief that moderation and reason could play decisive roles, even in the Arab world. When relations were at their worst between his own country (for he is an Egyptian) and such monarchies as

Saudi Arabia and Jordan, Hassouna remained *persona grata* with kings as well as presidents.

In the first month of 1964 a new crisis suddenly revitalized the League and restored Hassouna Pasha's import. Israel had threatened to divert, unilaterally, the waters of the river Jordan so as to water her southern desert. Faced with this threat a remarkable meeting took place. Every Arab head of state, with the exception of King Idris of Libya and President Shehab of Lebanon (who were ill), came to Cairo. The kings and presidents stayed in the Nile Hilton, which was cleared of all its guests. Each of the floors was shared by two heads of state. Egyptian army engineers improvised a closed corridor between the Hilton and the Arab League building. President Nasser treated the League property as extra-territorial; the discussions were chaired by President Aref of Iraq. The chief decisions of the summit meeting were directed towards uniting the Arabs by ending the chronic feuds that had divided them. Radio campaigns of abuse would be suspended.

The Arab League building adds an extra dimension to Cairo. The cliché of the Egyptians that 'Cairo is the heart of Arabism' seems true; the city on the Nile is an emotional focus to men and women from Morocco and Kuwait, Iraq and Yemen.

Another dimension is added by the Africans who have either made Cairo their basis for struggle, or who have returned as visiting heads of independent states. A whole quarter of Zamalek is dark with plotting nationalists; some of these Africans are suspicious of their host country, others ungrateful for its assistance; but all regard it as indispensable, the chief city of a continent in ferment.

Cairo is more than a market of quaint wares, more than a museum. It is an arena where some of the basic issues of the century are being fought out, sometimes with exaggeration, always with fervour. If this implies a touch of peril, it implies, too, that quickening nerve whose presence makes the difference between an excursion and an experience.

Index

Salocius.